Celebrate
HIGHLANDS

Recipes and Remembrance

THE
LAUREL GARDEN
CLUB

Celebrate
HIGHLANDS
Recipes and Remembrance

ISBN: 0-9709396-0-4

Designed, Edited, and Manufactured by
Favorite Recipes® Press
An imprint of

FRP

P. O. Box 305142
Nashville, Tennessee 37230
1-800-358-0560

Art Director: Steve Newman
Designer: Starletta Polster
Project Manager: Susan Larson

Manufactured in the United States of America
First Printing: 2002   5,000 copies
Second Printing: 2002   3,000 copies

Laurel Garden Club

Founded in 1982, the Laurel Garden Club
is dedicated to the protection and conservation
of Highlands' natural resources, its village
beauty, and its roadside charm. The club's purpose
is charitable and educational. Proceeds
from the sale of this book will benefit the Highlands
Botanical Gardens/Nature Center, as well
as other projects which are in agreement with
the club's stated purpose.

Dedication

This book is dedicated to all those people and
organizations that protect and preserve Highlands'
rich heritage, beauty, and natural environment.

Foreword

Celebrating Victuals (Pronounced Viddles) on the Highlands Plateau of Macon County, North Carolina

The editor of *Celebrate Highlands* must have known that a quirky writer like myself couldn't limit himself to 500 words—I can't clear my throat in 500 words. For writing to have any flavor it has to tell you something "interesting." A writer must be truly generous with the words, so the reader will want to "take two and butter them while they're hot."

Whenever I am presented with a literary task, I immediately open one of my favorite books, the monumental *New Dictionary of Quotations on Historical Principle from Ancient and Modern Sources,* selected and edited by H. L. Mencken (Alfred A. Knopf, New York, 1942). You see what masters have had to say on the subject. It always primes the word pump. When I began to scan the entries on "Cookery," I got a few jolts.

"It's a bad cook who can't lick his own fingers." An English proverb, very pungent, traced to circa 1520.

"Woman does not understand what food means, and yet she insists upon being a cook!" That is our learned, occasionally genial friend, Uncle Fred Nietzsche, really way out there on the far side of Lake Misogyny.

"When a cook cooks a fly he keeps the best wing for himself." A glorious Polish proverb that explains why we seldom eat Polish. And: "The discovery of a new dish does more for human happiness than the discovery of a new star." That is Anthelme Brillat-Savarin, from his amazing *Physiology of Taste* (1825).

That last one tells you what's wanted from a cookbook—something absolutely scrumptious; something as fresh as the new dawn. *Celebrate Highlands* offers a lot of interesting starters, lots of desirable entrées, and plenty of tasty desserts, designed for small, private, festive occasions. This is not complex cooking and you won't need to fly to Paris and study for a year. It is up-market and pleasingly casual at the same time. Also, much is said in texts of Highlands' past. The vignettes and sidebars are genuinely attractive. So are the drawings and Amelia James' cover.

Fifteen years ago our very small press, Jargon Books of Highlands, issued a book called *White Trash*

Cooking, by Earnest Matthew Mickler, a card-carrying White-Trash boy from North Florida. It had recipes for "Grand Canyon Cake" and "Tutti's Fruited Porkettes," "Rack of Spam," "Betty Sue's Sister-in-Law's Fried Eggplant," "Mona Lisa Sapp's Macaroni Salad," "The Kitchen Sink Tomato Sandwich," and "Russian Communist Tea Cakes." The Nation belched loudly and then got ready to buy nearly a million copies. Governor Jim Hunt liked it and said if you are what you eat, then he was White Trash all his life and didn't know it until now.

All this was fun for awhile but we soon realized that we weren't big enough to cope with a book that actually "sold." Ten Speed Press bought *White Trash Cooking* and has done a great job of placing it in airports, bookstores, and nearly everywhere else. (One recipe from *White Trash Cooking* has been snuck into *Celebrate Highlands;* after all, the publisher—no cook—lives here.) But I hope that *Celebrate Highlands* stays right here in Macon County and that local chefs work their culinary skills on their home ground. These are gatherings for friends and families with the seasonal, local life of Highlands setting the stage.

Another tangent: think back to the 1940s (those who can). About the only "eating out" to be done in Highlands was Sunday dinner at the Potts House (now the nicely restored Main Street Inn). Mrs. Charlie Potts (aka "Madame Queen") provided delicious chicken and dumplings, plus very fresh vegetables, breads, salads, fruits, and desserts. Later on, in "The Highlander" restaurant Mary Thompson's Buttermilk Pie became the obsession of many. And people still track Ruby Vinson from restaurant to restaurant to taste her pastries. Many of us will not forget that for over fifty years one of the very best things in Highlands was Elizabeth Edwards' Condiment Shop. I wonder how many jars of Onion Relish and Highlands Red Hot I have devoured over the decades? She was a master.

The traditional Anglo-Saxon food was good then and it's good today. But now of course, we have an enormous diversity to add to the traditional tastes. Salsa has triumphed over catsup. Lemon grass grows along the banks of Alph, the Sacred River. White people have learned to eat what black people, brown people, red people, and yellow people eat.

The French say: "Bon appétit!" What do we zestful Americans say? Maybe, *Put the sassafras and the sourwood honey on the sushi and let's Celebrate Highlands!*

—Jonathan Williams

Preface

Tucked into the corner of Western North Carolina on a plateau nearly 4,000 feet high in the heart of the Blue Ridge, the town of Highlands nestles on the north side of Satulah Mountain. It is not a large town. In the wintertime there are only 900 people, but in the summer the population of the area expands to over 20,000, with people enjoying the climate, scenery, varied shops, and remarkable diversity of flora. The mountains that surround Highlands are among the oldest in the world and in early days were home to the Cherokee Indians. The Cherokees had a name for Highlands: *Onteeorah,* Hills of the Sky. Many of the names of our mountains and rivers come from the Cherokee.

The first white men, traders, moved through these mountains in the 1600s, but the earliest settlers arrived in the late 1700s to farm in the coves below the plateau. In 1875 Samuel Kelsey and Clinton Hutchinson learned of the plateau, recognized its potential, and founded a town. It was highly advertised for its healthful climate, and people came. They have been coming ever since. Some leave for the winter season but soon return. For whether it is hiking up a mountain, walking in the forest fastness, enjoying a chamber music concert or a community play, meeting old friends, sitting beside a waterfall, playing in a river, searching out the unique plants and trees of our area, reminiscing about old times, or basking in the sunset's glow, residents and visitors alike glory in this unique and wonderful place. They enjoy the freshness and excitement of its "now" and the nostalgia of its "then." They Celebrate Highlands in many ways: with music, art, writing, and with talented contributions to the community.

Many of the celebrations in Highlands today are embellished by food. A century ago, Highlanders were dependent on what they could raise at home or hunt in the forest or catch in the rivers. Reaching this small hamlet then was not an easy task, for there were few roads. Today, people from all around the nation and foreign countries visit our community, bringing with them new culinary skills, ideas, and tastes. Our restaurant chefs and caterers set a high standard. Highlands' taste and dining expectations have come of age.

Please join with us, the Laurel Garden Club, and celebrate with exciting food the exquisite beauty, biodiversity, and special occasions of our Highlands' mountains.

Table of Contents

Rosemary Is for Remembrance   8

Laurel Garden Club Members   10

Menus & Celebrations   11

Appetizers & Beverages   39

Soups, Salads & Vegetables   57

Entrées   77

Pasta, Grains & Breads   97

Eggs, Cheese & Brunch   107

Desserts   115

Celebrity Chefs & Off the Mountain   129

Acknowledgements   153

Bibliography   155

Index   156

Order Form   160

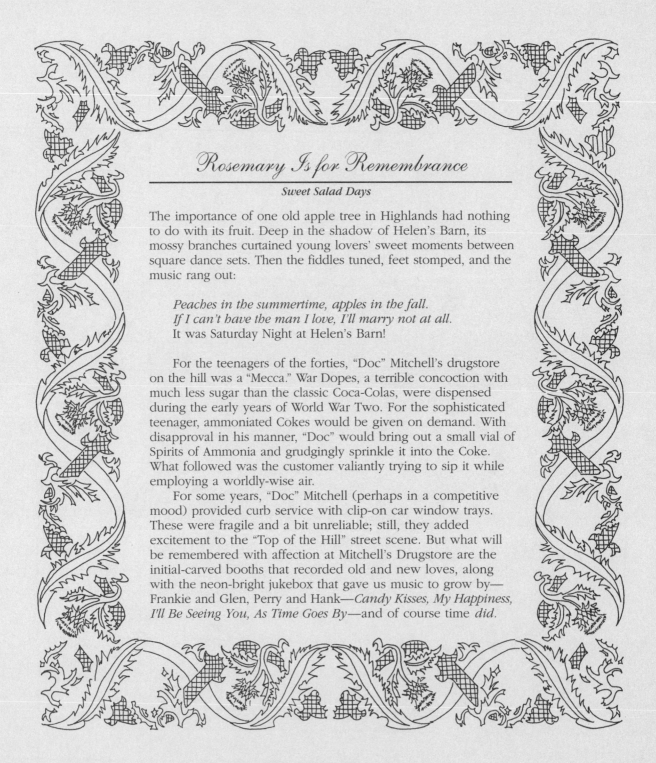

Rosemary Is for Remembrance

Sweet Salad Days

The importance of one old apple tree in Highlands had nothing to do with its fruit. Deep in the shadow of Helen's Barn, its mossy branches curtained young lovers' sweet moments between square dance sets. Then the fiddles tuned, feet stomped, and the music rang out:

Peaches in the summertime, apples in the fall.
If I can't have the man I love, I'll marry not at all.
It was Saturday Night at Helen's Barn!

For the teenagers of the forties, "Doc" Mitchell's drugstore on the hill was a "Mecca." War Dopes, a terrible concoction with much less sugar than the classic Coca-Colas, were dispensed during the early years of World War Two. For the sophisticated teenager, ammoniated Cokes would be given on demand. With disapproval in his manner, "Doc" would bring out a small vial of Spirits of Ammonia and grudgingly sprinkle it into the Coke. What followed was the customer valiantly trying to sip it while employing a worldly-wise air.

For some years, "Doc" Mitchell (perhaps in a competitive mood) provided curb service with clip-on car window trays. These were fragile and a bit unreliable; still, they added excitement to the "Top of the Hill" street scene. But what will be remembered with affection at Mitchell's Drugstore are the initial-carved booths that recorded old and new loves, along with the neon-bright jukebox that gave us music to grow by—Frankie and Glen, Perry and Hank—*Candy Kisses, My Happiness, I'll Be Seeing You, As Time Goes By*—and of course time *did*.

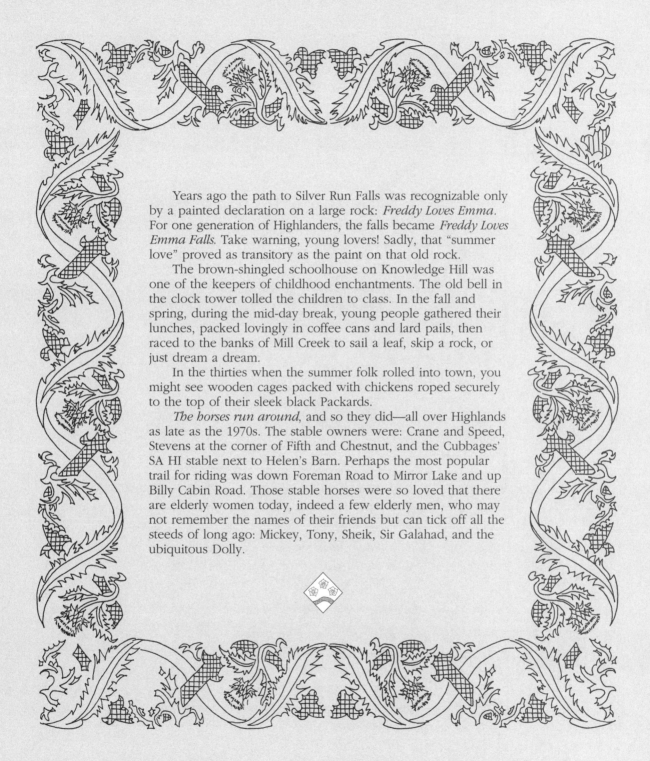

Years ago the path to Silver Run Falls was recognizable only by a painted declaration on a large rock: *Freddy Loves Emma*. For one generation of Highlanders, the falls became *Freddy Loves Emma Falls*. Take warning, young lovers! Sadly, that "summer love" proved as transitory as the paint on that old rock.

The brown-shingled schoolhouse on Knowledge Hill was one of the keepers of childhood enchantments. The old bell in the clock tower tolled the children to class. In the fall and spring, during the mid-day break, young people gathered their lunches, packed lovingly in coffee cans and lard pails, then raced to the banks of Mill Creek to sail a leaf, skip a rock, or just dream a dream.

In the thirties when the summer folk rolled into town, you might see wooden cages packed with chickens roped securely to the top of their sleek black Packards.

The horses run around, and so they did—all over Highlands as late as the 1970s. The stable owners were: Crane and Speed, Stevens at the corner of Fifth and Chestnut, and the Cubbages' SA HI stable next to Helen's Barn. Perhaps the most popular trail for riding was down Foreman Road to Mirror Lake and up Billy Cabin Road. Those stable horses were so loved that there are elderly women today, indeed a few elderly men, who may not remember the names of their friends but can tick off all the steeds of long ago: Mickey, Tony, Sheik, Sir Galahad, and the ubiquitous Dolly.

Laurel Garden Club Members

Judy Allison	Amelia James
Carol Avinger	Edith Joel
Glenda Bell	Ruth Layton
Jodi Benson-Zahner	Judith Mackie
Mary Berry	Elinor Metzger
Pat Boyd	Jane Mitchell
Sue Brigham	Kitty Moore
Millie Broughton	Madolyn Nickerson
Pat Buchanan	Jeune Orebaugh
Jean Clarke	Ute Partain
Mary Nell Clifton	Keturah Paulk
Beverly Coker	Virginia Reynaud
Jane Davis	Anna Rogers
Betty Dobson	Marie Sharpe
Anne Doggett	Sue Sheehan
Martha Dunson	Dottie Shepherd
Barbara Estes	Rosemary Stiefel
Jane FitzPatrick	Harriet Stone
Margo Franklin	Juliana Stottlemyer
Sandra Freeman	Lamira Sullivan
Sarah Fricks	Lyniece Talmadge
Rachel Hamilton	Nancy Tarbox
Mary Hardee	Joyce Tiller
Mary Eva Harper	Petey Clay Tully
Eleanor Harrison	Evalyn Turner
Betty Heery	Madeleine Watt
Mercedes Heller	Paulette Webb
Ann Herbert	Elaine Whitehurst
Bette Hester	Fran Young
Beverly Howell	Glenda Zahner

Menus & Celebrations

Buffet Menu

Greek Olive Tapenade with toasted French bread rounds

Cheddar Chili Cheesecake

Magnificent Marinated Chicken

Curried Rice Salad

Tomato Cucumber Platter with Feta

Roasted Sesame Asparagus

Country ham on Sage Cream Biscuits

Toffee Crunch Cookies

Welcome Back Buffet

Go shout it on the mountain!
"Our summer friends are back!"

It's May. The mountain laurel has burst into bloom, each blossom a cluster of tiny, pink-tinged teacups. Cloud upon cloud of pink and white decorate the mountainsides. The flame azalea is budding with shades of yellows and oranges to reds. The hummers have built their nests. Returning warblers and finches gladden our day with serenades.

The town bustles with excitement as shopkeepers plant window boxes, pots, and hanging baskets. Green and inviting, the golf courses sparkle. On the hill, the Playhouse actors are rehearsing. The Center for Life Enrichment is polishing up its programs. As our artists return, The Bascom-Louise Gallery shows grow more elaborate. The chamber music ensembles are tuning up their instruments.

Everywhere there are meetings. Highlands Historical Society has opened its doors to summer,

and the Highlands Biological Station is planning its speakers and programs. Special events and occasions are filling the season's calendar. Join us this evening in the fragrant Highlands' dusk to celebrate summertime.

Picnic Menus

Cooler Picnic

Traveling Soup

Roast Beef in Pita Pockets

Rainbow Pasta Salad

Pecan Bars

Seasonal fruit

Backpack Picnic

Chicken Cutlets with Lime

White Pimento Cheese with Crackers

Vidalia Onion Sandwiches

Mustard Coleslaw

Apple Brownies

Moveable Feasts

A picnic down in Walnut Cove,

A hike to Hurrah Ridge,

But there's one place you'll love the best:

Chattooga's Iron Bridge!

There's a magic on the Chattooga Loop in May when the early wildflowers bloom. Take time to enjoy trillium, jack-in-the-pulpit, the Clintonia lily, dainty, white hepatica, pink and yellow lady slippers. Overhead, lacy, white blossoms of serviceberry and silver bell make a show against the emerging greens of the forest.

On the broadest rock by the river, you'll want to spread a colorful quilt and unpack coolers filled with lemonade and chilled wine. Unload baskets of crusty bread and cheeses, fruits and sweet delicacies. Hand around large cloth napkins and generous glasses. Challenge the crowd to create a centerpiece in the empty basket of found things: pile up mosses, barks, lichens, driftwood, twisted roots, and smooth, polished stones from the river. While you're collecting, look sharp! The great blue heron may rise to flight. Another day, carry a moveable feast to Sunset Rock and make ceremony of a crimson sunset over Highlands. Linger through the mother-of-pearl afterglow until bright stars shine out. Don't forget a cushion, for you will be resting on the world's oldest and hardest rock.

Or picnic on a high mountain unencumbered with coolers. If it's spring, tuck an apple and a PB&J into your pack and be off. In winter, fill a small thermos with hot soup and celebrate a January thaw. Life is indeed a picnic in Highlands!

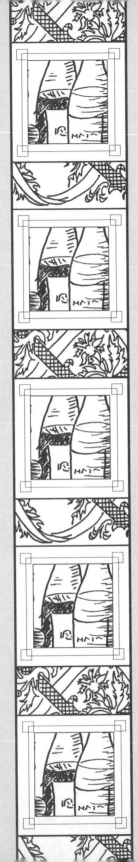

Twilight Golf Party

Fillet-Topped Baguettes

Caviar Spread

Chicken and Date Salad Canapés

Pesto Torta

Shrimp Mousse Mold

Antipasto Florida

U-Pick Tomato Sandwiches

Hot and Sweet Pecans

Twilight Golf

In the beginning, God, herself, created the mountains and the forests.

Next, Kelsey and Hutchinson designed the town.

And on the seventh day, Bobby Jones laid out a golf course.

Honey, get my jacket....Are the clubs on the cart?" It's time for Twilight Golf, a weekly four-ball event to be followed by a backyard buffet. Some call it "Hit and Giggle," because semipros and backyard duffers are all mixed up together. Fellowship seems to be the goal of twilight golf.

Hearty casseroles, crisp salads, and luscious dips are already prepared and waiting in the fridge. Or maybe a steak is marinating. After the game, the losers will have to crank the ice cream. But for now, put your mind on golf. Tee up your ball and give it your very best shot. Golf rules in Highlands.

Dinner Menu

Tortilla Pinwheels

Baked Mexican Spinach Dip with Tortilla Chips

Grilled Swordfish with Avocado Butter

Cucumber Ring

Highlands Tomato Pie

Peach Rum Soufflé

Alfresco Dinner

"Come early," the handwritten invitation says, "and we'll stroll through the garden. The sun slants through the tall trees just so at this time of year lighting up the lilies and delphinium and making tree shadows and pools of sunlight on the lawn." Who could resist such an invitation?

At the appointed hour, women in lovely trailing gowns and shawls and shoulder-grazing earrings and golf-tanned men in colorful open-necked shirts and blazers or pale, striped "ice cream" suits move through the gardens. They stop and start like butterflies visiting the kaleidoscope of blossoms. The sharp fragrance of new-mown grass mixes with the perfume of nicotiana and peonies and heliotrope. Laughter happens easily as the western sky turns to pink. Then dusk and fireflies.

Small tables, draped in grass-length linens, scatter about the lawn.

Chippendale chairs, brought out from the dining room for this special occasion, seem startled at their new surroundings. Ice cubes frozen with violets, lemon slices, and strawberries tinkle in the crystal goblets. The host, making a ceremony of lighting each candle, begins the song…

"Now the day is over…"

A baritone supports the melody,

"…night is drawing nigh…"

Other voices join in, *"Shadows of the evening move across the sky…."*

Even in Highlands, it just doesn't get any better than this.

Backyard Supper

Chinese Chicken Wings

Grilled Flank Steak with Black Bean and Corn Salsa

Mustard Coleslaw

Tomatoes Stuffed with Squash

Peach Ice Cream

Almond Cookies

Spicy Iced Tea

A Backyard Summer Afternoon

"Lemonade, made in the shade,
stirred with a spade, Pink Lemonade…"

Listen! Is that the clink of ice and horseshoes? Fill up your backyard with friends and family. Set up the croquet court and pile the hammock high with pillows. Arrange a three-legged race. Make daisy chains and braid flowers and ribbon in the hair of little girls. Add bruised mint to the drinks and basil to the bouquets of roses, snapdragons, and delphinium.

While toddlers play in the sprinkler and babies sleep on pale quilts beneath the trees, arrange sawhorses and planks into a rustic table.

Then serve up your heartiest picnic fare: great platters of soft pink ham and red tomatoes and sharp green pickles and golden cheesy casseroles. Followed by shirt-staining blueberry/ blackberry cobblers, all washed down with lemonade and minty tea.

As dusk comes on, the little ones will chase the lightning bugs; uncles will groan and rise to a challenge from the teenagers to a game of horseshoes. The long afternoon slides easily into evening.

At dusk your party will be blessed by the lyric of the whippoorwill and by the question of nearby neighbor owls as they wonder back and forth in owl-speak: "whooo… whooo… whooo cooks for yooou?"

Menu for an "Afters" Supper

Brie with Sun-Dried Tomatoes

Belvedere Mushroom Almond Pâté with melba rounds

Salmon with Arugula, Tomato and Caper Sauce

Pasta with Sugar Snap Peas, Asparagus and Parmesan

Chamber Music Sundaes

Schubert Supper

The invitation reads:
"An Afters Supper! Join us 'after' feasting on Schubert's Trout Quintet
at the Performing Arts Center."

It's July and our mountains are alive with the sound of music: music sweeter to the ear than the roar of waterfalls, the sound of the wind in the pines, and the song of rivers. Sweeter than fiddle music, bagpipes, and the Presbyterian Chimes. Chamber music has returned once again to Highlands as it has for more than twenty years. It is our season to be enlightened, entertained, and moved by the talents of world-renowned festival artists.

So celebrate the event by adorning your table with gleaming silver, crisp white linens, and antique china. Cut the heavy-headed July flowers in your garden. Make bouquets with brilliant-colored dahlias, stately yellow sunflowers, and glorious oriental lilies. Food? Ah, little matter, for surely tonight you have dined on ambrosia and drunk the nectar of the gods!

Allegro vivace

A Celtic Lunch

Brie with Apricot Spread

Poached Salmon and Pasta with Cucumber Dressing

Spicy Tomato Aspic

Matchstick Vegetables with Lemon Thyme Butter

Sweet Potato Biscuits

Cold Lemon Soufflé

Kirkin' O' the Tartan

"You are invited to lift your banners

and sing that fine old hymn,

Amazing Grace."

At the Kirkin' o' the Tartan, burly pipers on sturdy legs, clothed in bright and muted tartan kilts, knee socks, and bonnets, march in deliberate procession down the aisle of the Episcopal or Presbyterian Church. The eerie, plaintive strains of bagpipe music swirl around the worshippers. MacGregors and Campbells and Burns and Moores all carry their banners proudly, paying homage to their Scottish ancestry. Today, everyone claims to have a Scotsman in his heritage.

If you are lucky enough to be invited to a Celtic meal after the Kirkin' and have a little bit of a brogue, you might be asked by your host to return the blessing. Here's a wonderful one. It is the Selkirk Grace brought to us by the poet Robbie Burns:

Some hae meat and canna eat,

And some wad eat that want it;

But we hae meat, and we can eat,

And sae the Lord be thankit.

"Amen"

Moonlight Dinner

Crab-Stuffed Mushrooms

Sun-Dried Tomato Pesto and Shrimp Bruschetta

Smoked Salmon on Salad Greens

Bleu Cheese Tomato Soup

Petit filet with Tabasco Mayonnaise

Portobello Mushroom Stacks

Whipped Potatoes with Garlic and Chives

Raspberry Walnut Torte

Full Moon Dinner

"I see the moon, the moon sees me…"

Decorate your outdoor table with silver candlesticks and gleaming goblets. Arrange the fragrant and pale blossoms of peonies and lilies and antique roses. Serve Champagne and caviar. Drape soft shawls across the arms of chairs against the later coolness of the evening.

Watch moon shadows steal across the lawn.
Get giddy on the moonlight.

Flirt a little.

Strum a mandolin and sing *moon* songs.
"The moon sees the one…that I want to see…"

But watch out for that moonshine.
"God bless the moon and God bless me…."

The effect is more intoxicating than the finest Champagne!
"And God bless the one that I want to see."

Fall Dinner Menu

Bleu Cheese and Roasted Walnuts

Mountain Trout (Three Ways)

Cold Oriental Loin of Pork with Horseradish Applesauce

Colcannon (Cabbage and Potatoes)

Herb Baked Tomatoes

Apple Harvest Cake

October Outing

Autumn is the distillation of our long, sweet mountain summer into perfection. A perfect pumpkin, a perfect McIntosh, buckberry, or prickly chinquapin. A black gum leaf, a hornet's nest. A cabbage. A persimmon.

Notice the changing color of the hardwoods as first the reds, then the yellows creep down the mountains. Take to the woods with a grandchild and your tree book. Press some leaves between the pages and pass on the wonder. Enjoy the purple weeds of fall: joe-pye, ironweed, and the mysterious closed purple gentian.

You will ALWAYS have houseguests in autumn, and they won't have brought any proper hiking shoes, so take them on an auto tour. At Dendy's Orchard, stock up on freshly harvested local apples and cider. At Scaly Mountain, steal a nice fresh cabbage or a pumpkin (just kidding). At the very end of the beautiful Betty's Creek Valley of Rabun County, let your guests pull their own fish from Andy's heavily stocked Trout Pond. Stop by Barker's Mill, behind the Hambidge Center and get some cornmeal. You'll want to make hushpuppies to go with those trout.

Back home, put on some Merle Haggard or maybe some Mozart and set your friends to work peeling apples for a pie and quartering cabbage for a creamy, cheesy casserole like the Dillards down in Rabun County taught us how to make. Let the boldest one carve the pumpkin into a grinning jack-o'-lantern while you grill sausages and those fresh-caught mountain trout. Spice up some cider and encourage the crowd to compose a litany of your shared autumnal blessings.

Brunch After the Christmas Parade

Swedish Glögg

Artichoke Rarebit over toast points

Giddy Up Grits

Apricot Casserole

Cranberries and Cream Bread

Christmas Parade

Grab a cup of coffee and find a good watching place along Main Street. Here comes the band; the Highlands Christmas parade is about to begin! Sometimes the parade leads off with the fire truck, siren wailing. Sometimes it's a cotton-cloud-covered white pick-up truck stuffed with angels. Once it was the scrubbed, sterilized and be-ribboned sanitation truck. But no matter who leads off, it *always* ends with Santa Claus, because when he's not at his summer home at the North Pole, he's a taxpaying resident of our town.

Wave at the high school celebrities. Scramble with the youngsters for the candies thrown by uniformed Boy Scouts and civic groups. Marvel at the rally of beautifully restored antique automobiles, show-off horses in fancy tack, and overalled, moonshine-flavored mountaineers clowning for the crowd. Then goats and a donkey and a gaggle of classy dogs with curly tails. Anything goes in the Christmas parade, including the spirited ladies of the Mountain Garden Club who march in costume. They stop the show three or four times along the way to perform a routine, such as "Lettuce hoe, lettuce hoe, lettuce hoe."

Wave goodbye to Santa Claus and hurry to meet friends and neighbors for a festive Christmas brunch. "'Tis the season to be *JOLLY.*"

Feliz Navidad

Mexican Shrimp

Black Bean Dip with tortilla chips

Chicken Tortilla Soup

Hot Chile Quesadillas

Fabulous Flan

Oh, Christmas Tree

Be as a child again at the lighting of the town's gigantic Christmas tree. Make believe this is the very first Christmas tree lighting you have ever seen, and certainly the most beautiful. Wait for dark to fall, and sing around the unlit tree of other *Midnights Clear* and *Tannenbaums*. Little boys hold out mittened hands to catch the imagined snowflakes. Dogs bark and chase one another, and perhaps the moon comes up.

When Santa throws the magic switch, the tree of Christmas comes alive with great globe lights of every color. Little boys cheer and whistle, old men stomp their feet. With shining eyes, you clasp hands and sing, "O, Little Town of Bethlehem, / How still we see thee lie." And you are filled with thankfulness for the One whose birth we celebrate and with love for those who share this experience in your very own little town of Highlands.

Suddenly you're overtaken with a great hunger and imagine you can smell the stews and soups and gingerbread wafting from kitchens all over town. Call out good wishes. Wave goodbye, and hurry home to share supper with friends and sing more carols around a crackling fire.

Cabin Fever Supper

Cabin Onion Soufflé

Southwestern Soup

Almond and Orange Salad

Sour Cream Corn Bread

Fig Preserve Cake

Cabin Fever

Sometimes it happens....The wind blows out of the north and the temperature drops twenty degrees in an hour. The snow begins in friendly soft flakes. You replenish your inside firewood supply and pull your easy chair up to the window. Wow, this is really something! It keeps on, and the flakes keep getting bigger. First, the mountain is obscured. Then the barn. Then the garden. Dusk falls really early. Gathering your knitting and your books, you turn on the radio and settle in for a pleasant evening.

Then the power goes off. Cabin Fever usually sets in within twenty-four hours.

There's another kind of "cabin fever." That's when your houseguests get snowed in with you and can't go home on Sunday afternoon as planned, and the power goes out. (This is the worst kind of cabin fever.) Monday morning they are *really* cold, having brought only designer cotton sweaters and Frederick's of Hollywood nighties. Why won't the toilet flush? they wonder, having no understanding of pumps and things. But after a breakfast of eggs scrambled on the Coleman stove and toast scorched on the poker over the fire, things look a little brighter.

You play bridge all morning with two tables pulled up really close to the fireplace. Firewood is going fast. The bedrooms, by now, are like ICE. Cold leftovers and peanut butter sandwiches are acceptable for lunch—amusing even. Guests slip to the telephone (the only thing that works, one says) to call their offices. Cocktail hour begins *immediately* after lunch.

In preparation for supper, you put the leftover leftovers in a large pot on the tiny burner of the Coleman stove with some chicken stock and whatever else the freezer gives up.

You pray the propane will hold out. The host prays the whiskey will hold out. The guests pray the snowplow will come. And it's still snowing.

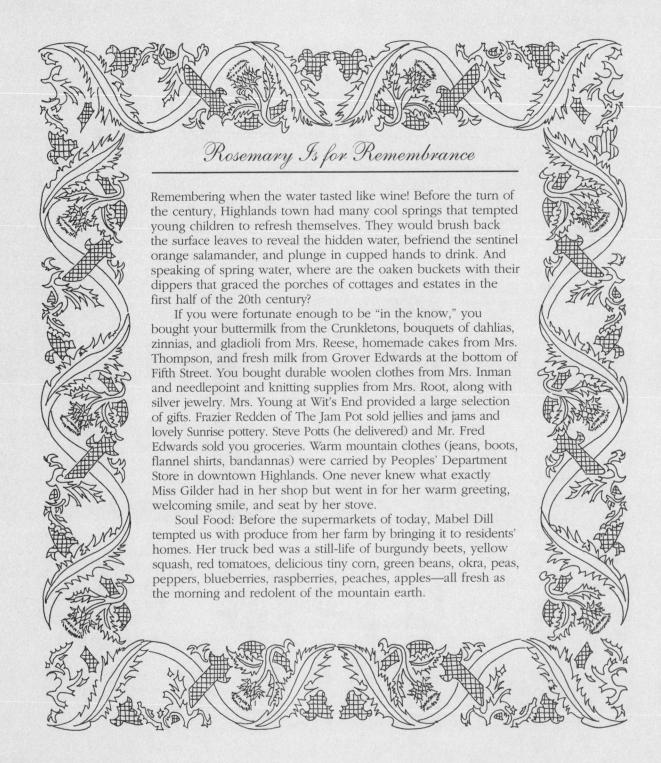

Rosemary Is for Remembrance

Remembering when the water tasted like wine! Before the turn of the century, Highlands town had many cool springs that tempted young children to refresh themselves. They would brush back the surface leaves to reveal the hidden water, befriend the sentinel orange salamander, and plunge in cupped hands to drink. And speaking of spring water, where are the oaken buckets with their dippers that graced the porches of cottages and estates in the first half of the 20th century?

If you were fortunate enough to be "in the know," you bought your buttermilk from the Crunkletons, bouquets of dahlias, zinnias, and gladioli from Mrs. Reese, homemade cakes from Mrs. Thompson, and fresh milk from Grover Edwards at the bottom of Fifth Street. You bought durable woolen clothes from Mrs. Inman and needlepoint and knitting supplies from Mrs. Root, along with silver jewelry. Mrs. Young at Wit's End provided a large selection of gifts. Frazier Redden of The Jam Pot sold jellies and jams and lovely Sunrise pottery. Steve Potts (he delivered) and Mr. Fred Edwards sold you groceries. Warm mountain clothes (jeans, boots, flannel shirts, bandannas) were carried by Peoples' Department Store in downtown Highlands. One never knew what exactly Miss Gilder had in her shop but went in for her warm greeting, welcoming smile, and seat by her stove.

Soul Food: Before the supermarkets of today, Mabel Dill tempted us with produce from her farm by bringing it to residents' homes. Her truck bed was a still-life of burgundy beets, yellow squash, red tomatoes, delicious tiny corn, green beans, okra, peas, peppers, blueberries, raspberries, peaches, apples—all fresh as the morning and redolent of the mountain earth.

The first telephone office was located next to The Old
Edwards Inn on Fourth Street and was one of the most popular
places in town. As late as 1942, only a handful of people owned
a telephone. The operator, or "central," of that day was Manilla
Reese Rhodes. While waiting to call, one overheard interesting
tidbits of gossip and friendships were forged forever.

Harry Holt's Western Union Office and taxi was located next
to brother Bill Holt's Soda Shop on the corner of Fourth and
Main. Within close proximity to the telephone office, Harry could
act on an urgent phone call to "central" (Manilla) or deliver
telegrams. It was always a little frightening, particularly during
World War II years, to see Harry's old black car, brownish beige
most days from muddy roads, lumber into your yard.

Few Highlanders born in the early half of the 20th century
are likely to forget the era of handmade advertisements for local
shops, services, and horse stables displayed in the old movie
theater. The advertisements (sometimes just rough lettering)
appeared to be pulled across the screen before the movie began
or shown during the frequent changing of a reel or breakdown.
The musical accompaniment was a fitful and tinny rendition of
Bless Them All followed by *The Blue Danube Waltz.* Either tune
heard today transports those elderly Highlanders instantly to that
darkened room where magic was dispensed.

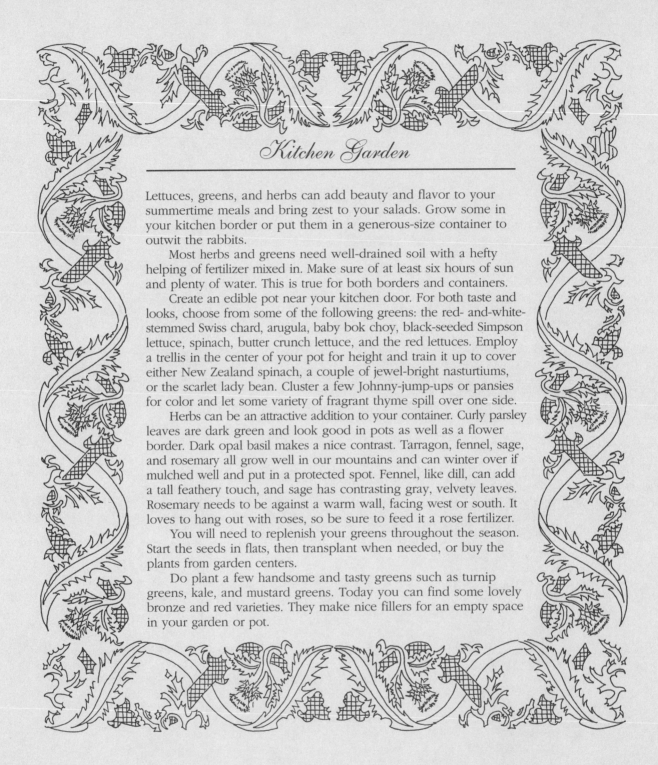

Kitchen Garden

Lettuces, greens, and herbs can add beauty and flavor to your summertime meals and bring zest to your salads. Grow some in your kitchen border or put them in a generous-size container to outwit the rabbits.

Most herbs and greens need well-drained soil with a hefty helping of fertilizer mixed in. Make sure of at least six hours of sun and plenty of water. This is true for both borders and containers.

Create an edible pot near your kitchen door. For both taste and looks, choose from some of the following greens: the red- and-white-stemmed Swiss chard, arugula, baby bok choy, black-seeded Simpson lettuce, spinach, butter crunch lettuce, and the red lettuces. Employ a trellis in the center of your pot for height and train it up to cover either New Zealand spinach, a couple of jewel-bright nasturtiums, or the scarlet lady bean. Cluster a few Johnny-jump-ups or pansies for color and let some variety of fragrant thyme spill over one side.

Herbs can be an attractive addition to your container. Curly parsley leaves are dark green and look good in pots as well as a flower border. Dark opal basil makes a nice contrast. Tarragon, fennel, sage, and rosemary all grow well in our mountains and can winter over if mulched well and put in a protected spot. Fennel, like dill, can add a tall feathery touch, and sage has contrasting gray, velvety leaves. Rosemary needs to be against a warm wall, facing west or south. It loves to hang out with roses, so be sure to feed it a rose fertilizer.

You will need to replenish your greens throughout the season. Start the seeds in flats, then transplant when needed, or buy the plants from garden centers.

Do plant a few handsome and tasty greens such as turnip greens, kale, and mustard greens. Today you can find some lovely bronze and red varieties. They make nice fillers for an empty space in your garden or pot.

Appetizers & Beverages

Black Bean Dip

1 (16-ounce) can black beans
2 tablespoons chopped green onions
1 or 2 garlic cloves
1/2 teaspoon dill
2 tablespoons rice vinegar
1 tablespoon lime juice
Dash of cayenne pepper

Purée the undrained black beans, green onions, garlic, dill, rice vinegar, lime juice and cayenne pepper in a blender until smooth. Spoon into a serving bowl. Serve with tortilla chips.

Yield: 8 servings

Caviar Spread

2 (14-ounce) cans artichoke hearts
3/4 (8-ounce) bottle Italian salad dressing
2 (2-ounce) jars black caviar
1/4 cup (or more) mayonnaise
1 cup chopped fresh parsley

Drain the artichoke hearts and squeeze out the moisture. Chop the artichoke hearts finely. Arrange in a serving dish or mound on a tray or platter. Drizzle with the salad dressing. Layer the caviar over the artichoke hearts. Spread the mayonnaise over the top to cover. Sprinkle with the parsley. Serve with melba rounds or crackers.

Yield: 8 servings

The picturesque ruin of J. J. Smith's old red gristmill on Fourth Street is gone now. It once spanned Mill Creek where Sweet Treats is today.

40

White Pimento Cheese with Crackers

2 (4-ounce) jars chopped pimentos
1 pound white sharp Cheddar cheese, grated
2 tablespoons minced purple onion
1 bunch green onions, chopped
1 or 2 garlic cloves, minced
1 cup mayonnaise

Drain the pimentos and pat dry with paper towels. Combine the cheese, purple onion, green onions, garlic, pimentos and mayonnaise in the order listed in a bowl and mix well. Store, covered, in the refrigerator for several weeks. Use as a spread for crackers or use to make sandwiches.

Yield: 8 servings

Baked Mexican Spinach Dip with Tortilla Chips

1 (10-ounce) package frozen chopped spinach, thawed
1 cup chopped onion
2 tablespoons vegetable oil
3 medium tomatoes, peeled, seeded, chopped
2 tablespoons chopped jalapeños
2 cups shredded Monterey Jack cheese
4 ounces nonfat cream cheese, cut into 1/2-inch cubes
1 cup half-and-half
1/2 cup sliced black olives
1 tablespoon red wine vinegar
Salt and pepper to taste
1/2 cup shredded Monterey Jack cheese
Tortilla chips

Drain the spinach, squeezing out the excess moisture. Sauté the onion in the oil in a skillet until transparent. Add 2/3 of the tomatoes and chiles. Sauté for 2 minutes. Spoon into a large bowl. Add the spinach, 2 cups Monterey Jack cheese, cream cheese, half-and-half, black olives, red wine vinegar, salt and pepper and mix well. Spoon into a 11/2-quart baking dish. Bake at 400 degrees for 35 minutes or until hot and bubbly. Sprinkle with 1/2 cup Monterey Jack cheese and the remaining tomatoes. Serve with tortilla chips.

Yield: 8 servings

Sweet-smelling lavender makes a beautiful bouquet with a mint green ribbon around it. It would be a nice thing to take to one confined to the hospital.

In Greek mythology, Prometheus brought fire from heaven to earth on a fennel stem. The herb is a symbol of strength and has large yellow flowers from March through June.

Anchovy paste can be bought in a tube like toothpaste. It keeps forever. Add a bit to cream cheese for a quick hors d'oeuvre or to salad dressing for a distinctive taste.

Olive Tapenade

1 cup pitted kalamata olives
1 cup fresh basil leaves
6 canned anchovy fillets
2 garlic cloves, crushed
2 tablespoons capers, drained
1 tablespoon fresh lemon juice
1/2 cup light mayonnaise
Salt and pepper to taste

Process the olives, basil, anchovy fillets, garlic, capers and lemon juice in a food processor until blended. Add the mayonnaise and mix well. Season with salt and pepper to taste. Chill, covered, until ready to serve. You may store in the refrigerator for up to 3 days. Serve with bite-sized fresh vegetables or crostini.

Yield: 1 1/3 cups

Sherry Cheese Pâté

6 ounces cream cheese, softened
1 cup shredded sharp Cheddar cheese
2 tablespoons dry sherry
1/2 teaspoon curry powder
1/4 teaspoon salt
Major Grey's mango chutney to taste
Chopped green onions to taste

Combine the cream cheese, Cheddar cheese, sherry, curry powder and salt in a bowl and mix well. Shape into a rectangle about 1/2 inch thick on a serving platter. Cover with chutney. Sprinkle with green onions. Serve with assorted crackers.

Yield: 8 servings

Belvedere Mushroom Almond Pâté

1 cup almonds
12 ounces mushrooms
1 garlic clove, chopped
1 small onion, chopped
1/4 cup (1/2 stick) butter
3/4 teaspoon salt
1/2 teaspoon thyme
1/8 teaspoon white pepper
2 tablespoons canola oil

Toast the almonds on a baking sheet. Remove from the oven to cool. Process the mushrooms in a food processor until coarsely chopped. Sauté the garlic and onion in the butter in a skillet until the onion is transparent. Add the mushrooms, salt, thyme and white pepper and mix well. Cook until most of the liquid is evaporated.

Process the toasted almonds in a food processor until coarsely chopped. Reserve 2 tablespoons of the coarsely chopped almonds. Continue to process the remaining almonds to form a paste. Add the canola oil and process until creamy. Add the mushroom mixture and process until smooth. Stir in the reserved almonds. Pack into a mold. Chill, covered, for 8 to 12 hours. To serve, unmold onto a serving platter. Serve with Belvedere "Floodgate Vineyard" Pinot Noir.

Yield: 4 servings

Thyme was once burned as incense. Today it is used on roasted chicken and potatoes with olive oil.

Brie with Apricot Spread

1/2 cup water
1/4 cup chopped dried apricots
2 teaspoons brandy
1 (15-ounce) round Brie cheese
2 tablespoons chopped pecans

Combine the water, apricots and brandy in a saucepan. Bring to a boil over medium heat. Cook for 5 minutes or until the apricots are tender, stirring constantly. Remove the rind from the Brie cheese. Arrange the cheese on a baking sheet. Spread with the apricot mixture. Sprinkle with the pecans. Broil 8 inches from the heat source for 2 to 4 minutes or until the Brie cheese is soft. Arrange on a serving platter. Serve with gingersnaps or lightly sweetened crackers.

Yield: 8 to 10 servings

Brie with Sun-Dried Tomatoes

1 (16-ounce) round Brie cheese, chilled
4 oil-pack sun-dried tomatoes
6 garlic cloves, minced
2 tablespoons minced fresh parsley
2 tablespoons freshly grated Parmesan cheese
1 teaspoon crumbled basil, or 4 fresh basil leaves, snipped

Remove the rind from the Brie cheese. Arrange the cheese on a serving plate. Drain the sun-dried tomatoes, reserving 1 tablespoon of the oil. Mince the sun-dried tomatoes. Mash the garlic in a small bowl to form a paste. Add the sun-dried tomatoes, parsley, Parmesan cheese and basil and mix well. Add the reserved oil and mix well. Spread over the Brie cheese to cover. Let stand at room temperature for 1 hour before serving. Serve with French bread or crackers.

Yield: 6 to 8 servings

Sun-Dried Tomato and Goat Cheese Spread

2 ounces sun-dried tomatoes
5 1/2 ounces fresh goat cheese
1/2 teaspoon chopped fresh basil
Salt and pepper to taste

Soak the sun-dried tomatoes in water to cover in a small bowl at room temperature for 1 hour; drain. Process in a food processor until puréed. Add the goat cheese. Process until creamy. Add the basil, salt and pepper and mix well. Spoon into a serving bowl. Serve with specialty crackers or rosemary and garlic flatbread.

Yield: 12 servings

Note: You may substitute summer fresh tomatoes for the sun-dried tomatoes.

Cabin Onion Soufflé

8 ounces cream cheese, softened
1/4 cup mayonnaise
1 cup finely chopped onion
1 cup grated Parmesan cheese

Combine the cream cheese and mayonnaise in a bowl and mix well. Stir in the onion and Parmesan cheese. Spoon into a baking dish. Bake at 350 degrees for 15 to 20 minutes or until brown and bubbly. Serve with assorted crackers.

Yield: 8 to 10 servings

The "Play" was the thing for the Highlands' community in the last few years of the forties and early fifties. The wonderful Highlands Community Theater was created in the thirties by Jack and Virginia Wilcox, Tom FitzPatrick, and many other brilliant and interesting people. It was, however, a glorious entertainment and education due to the remarkable talents of Fred Coney Allen. Selecting from many of the popular Broadway plays of the thirties, forties, and fifties, along with a sampling of Molière and Chekhov, Fred inculcated in young and old players and play-goers an interest and love for theater magic that would last a lifetime.

Pesto Torta

8 ounces cream cheese, softened
1/2 cup (1 stick) butter, softened
2 tablespoons sun-dried tomatoes, chopped
1/2 cup pesto
Fresh basil

Cut a square of cheesecloth to fit a 2-cup plain or charlotte mold. Moisten the cheesecloth with water. Squeeze out excess moisture. Line the mold smoothly with the damp cheesecloth. Beat the cream cheese and butter in a mixing bowl until smooth and creamy. Alternate layers of the cream cheese mixture, sun-dried tomatoes and pesto in the prepared mold until all of the ingredients are used, ending with the cream cheese mixture. Fold the ends of the cheesecloth over the layers and press lightly to compact. Chill, covered, for 8 to 12 hours. Invert onto a serving dish and gently remove from the mold. Remove the cheesecloth. Garnish with basil. Serve with assorted crackers.

Yield: 8 to 10 servings

Fillet-Topped Baguettes

2/3 cup chopped fresh Italian parsley
1/2 cup chopped walnuts, toasted
1/2 cup grated Parmesan cheese
1/3 cup packed fresh basil
1 large garlic clove
1/2 cup (scant) extra-virgin olive oil
Salt to taste
1 pound fillet of beef, cooked rare, chilled
1 French baguette, cut into 1/2-inch slices

Process the parsley, walnuts, Parmesan cheese, basil and garlic in a food processor fitted with a steel blade. Add the olive oil gradually, processing constantly to form a smooth paste. Add salt and process until blended. Chill, covered, for 8 to 10 hours or freeze for up to 2 weeks.

Cut the beef into thin slices. Arrange a mound of the beef on each bread slice. Top with some of the pesto. Arrange on a serving platter. Serve immediately.

Yield: 8 to 10 servings

Traditionally made by hand in a mortar, pesto comes from the verb pestare, *meaning "to pound." Northern Italians make pesto using a variety of herbs, nuts, and anchovies. Try making pesto of arugula, anchovies, and olive oil. It's intense and fantastic.*

46

Shrimp Mousse Mold

1¹/₂ envelopes unflavored gelatin
¹/₂ cup cold water
1 (10-ounce) can tomato soup
8 ounces cream cheese, softened
1 cup mayonnaise
1 cup finely chopped celery
1 tablespoon finely chopped green onions
1 pound boiled shrimp, peeled, cut into small pieces
Salt and pepper to taste
12 dashes of Tabasco sauce, or to taste

Soften the gelatin in the cold water in a small bowl. Bring the soup to a boil in a saucepan, stirring constantly. Remove from the heat. Add the gelatin mixture and cream cheese. Beat until smooth and creamy. Add the mayonnaise and beat well. Stir in the remaining ingredients Pour into a mold. Chill, covered, until firm. Unmold onto a serving plate.

Yield: 8 to 10 servings

Note: You may pour into several small custard cups or molds to serve a smaller number of people and give some away.

Bacon Crisps

6 slices bacon, at room temperature
24 Waverly wafers

Cut the bacon slices into quarters; stretch slightly. Wrap 1 bacon quarter around each Waverly wafer. Arrange on a rack in a broiler pan. Bake at 225 degrees for 25 minutes; turn. Bake for 25 minutes longer.

Yield: 8 servings

Chicken and Date Salad Canapés

1 cup 1/4-inch cubes cooked chicken breasts
1/2 cup chopped pitted dates
1/4 cup chopped pecans
1/4 cup crumbled crisp bacon (4 slices)
1/2 cup mayonnaise
8 (or more) ribs endive

Combine the chicken, dates, pecans, bacon and mayonnaise in a bowl and mix well. Spread about 1 tablespoonful of the mixture on each rib endive.

Yield: 8 servings

Chinese Chicken Wings

36 chicken wings
1 cup soy sauce
1/2 cup sugar
1 cup packed dark brown sugar

Disjoint the wings and discard the tips. Arrange in a single layer in a baking pan. Combine the soy sauce, sugar and brown sugar in a bowl and mix well. Pour over the wings. Bake at 325 degrees for 30 minutes. Turn the wings. Bake for 30 minutes. Turn again. Bake for 20 minutes. Serve hot or at room temperature.

Yield: 6 servings

Crab-Stuffed Mushrooms

2 tablespoons butter
2 tablespoons flour
1 cup milk
2 pounds large button mushrooms or mushroom caps
1 (7-ounce) can crab meat, drained
1/4 cup undrained capers
2 cups seasoned bread crumbs
1/2 cup (1 stick) butter, melted
3 tablespoons grated Parmesan cheese
1/4 cup lemon juice

Melt 2 tablespoons butter in a saucepan. Stir in the flour. Add the milk gradually, stirring constantly. Cook until thickened, stirring constantly. Remove from the heat.

Clean the mushrooms, removing the stems if necessary. Arrange cap side up on a baking sheet. Combine the crab meat and capers in a bowl and mix well. Add the white sauce and 3/4 cup of the bread crumbs. Stuff into the mushroom caps. Combine the remaining 1 1/4 cups bread crumbs, 1/2 cup butter and Parmesan cheese in a bowl and mix well. Spoon over the top of the stuffed mushrooms. Drizzle with the lemon juice. Bake at 400 degrees for 10 minutes.

Yield: 8 servings

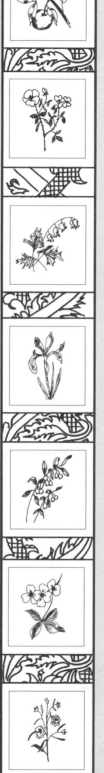

The Bascom-Louise Gallery is another Highlands' gem. Under the creative guidance of Ann Baird, it features interesting shows in many different mediums along with classes and activities for both young and old. Two of the highlights of the summer season, The Garden Tour of Homes and the lovely Bel Canto performance, benefit the Gallery.

Mexican Shrimp

2 pounds uncooked shrimp
1 large onion, sliced
3 garlic cloves, crushed
$1/2$ cup vegetable oil
3 large onions, sliced
Lemon juice
1 (4-ounce) can green chiles
$1/2$ cup vegetable oil
$1/2$ cup red wine vinegar
$1/2$ teaspoon dry mustard
Salt and pepper to taste
8 large tomatoes, peeled, sliced

Peel the shrimp and devein. Rinse the shrimp well. Sauté 1 onion and garlic in $1/2$ cup oil in a skillet until the onion is transparent. Add the shrimp. Stir-fry until the shrimp turn pink. Remove the shrimp to paper towels to drain. Let stand until cool.

Soak 3 onions in lemon juice to cover in a bowl. Drain the chiles, reserving the liquid. Cut the chiles into strips. Mix $1/2$ cup oil and red wine vinegar in a bowl. Add the reserved chile liquid, dry mustard, salt and pepper and blend well. Add the cooled shrimp. Marinate, covered, in the refrigerator until chilled. Drain the shrimp when ready to serve, discarding the marinade. Drain the onions, discarding the lemon juice. Arrange the shrimp on a serving platter. Arrange the drained onion slices, tomatoes and chile strips around the shrimp.

Yield: 8 to 10 servings

Sun-Dried Tomato Pesto and Shrimp Bruschetta

6 large handfuls basil leaves
3 tablespoons pine nuts
3 garlic cloves, crushed
1/4 cup grated Parmesan cheese
1/4 cup oil-pack sun-dried tomatoes
1/2 cup (about) olive oil
1 to 2 French baguettes
1 pound (35- to 40-count) shrimp, cooked, peeled,
    deveined

Process the basil leaves, pine nuts, garlic, Parmesan cheese, sun-dried tomatoes and olive oil in a food processor until mixed. Chill, covered, until ready to serve or for up to 24 hours. Cut the baguettes into slices. Arrange on a baking sheet. Bake at 350 degrees until light brown. Spread each baguette slice with 1 to 2 teaspoons of the pesto. Top each with 1 shrimp. Arrange on a serving platter.

Yield: 35 to 40 servings

Make your own grilled bread slices for bruschetta. Slice Italian or French bread about 1/2 inch thick. Brush with oil and grill or broil briefly. (You want the bread to still be soft on the inside.) Rub toasted bread with garlic. Turn the bread into bruschetta with the addition of a mixture of chopped tomatoes and basil with a touch of balsamic vinegar for flavor. Add a small slice of provolone and run it under the broiler. Or combine with dark olives or anchovies or other cheeses. A quick treat. Store the bread in an airtight container.

Antipasto Florida

8 ounces sliced fresh mushrooms
1 (14-ounce) can artichoke hearts, drained, finely chopped
1 (10-ounce) jar pimento-stuffed olives, drained, sliced
1 (6-ounce) can sliced black olives, drained
1/4 cup chopped green bell pepper
1/2 cup chopped celery
3/4 cup vinegar
3/4 cup virgin olive oil
1 teaspoon onion salt
1 teaspoon seasoned salt
1 teaspoon garlic salt
1 teaspoon sugar
1 teaspoon cracked pepper

Combine the mushrooms, artichoke hearts, pimento-stuffed olives, black olives, bell pepper and celery in a large bowl and toss to mix. Bring the vinegar, olive oil, onion salt, seasoned salt, garlic salt, sugar and pepper to a boil in a saucepan. Pour over the mushroom mixture. Spoon into a large jar with a tight-fitting lid. Cover with the lid and shake well. Chill for 8 to 12 hours. Drain the mushroom mixture, discarding the marinade. Arrange on a serving platter. Serve with wooden picks.

Yield: 8 to 10 servings

Smoked Salmon Appetizer Platter

3 ounces cream cheese
1 tablespoon drained capers
1 (3- or 4-ounce) package smoked salmon
1 cucumber, peeled, sliced
4 to 6 green onions
Melba rounds or miniature bagels

Place the cream cheese in the center of a serving plate. Top with the capers. Cut the salmon into strips. Arrange the salmon strips, cucumber slices and green onions around the cream cheese. Serve with melba rounds or miniature bagels.

Yield: 2 to 4 servings

Tortilla Pinwheels

3/4 cup drained canned black beans
3 ounces cream cheese, softened
2 teaspoons finely chopped jalapeños
8 (6-inch) flour tortillas
1 cup shredded Cheddar cheese
1/2 medium red bell pepper, finely chopped
4 green onions, chopped
Salsa or guacamole

Mash 1/2 cup of the black beans in a mixing bowl. Stir in
the remaining 1/4 cup whole black beans, cream cheese and
chiles. Spread over the tortillas. Sprinkle with the Cheddar
cheese, bell pepper and green onions. Roll up tightly. Wrap
in plastic wrap. Chill for 2 to 8 hours. Unwrap the roll-ups.
Cut into slices 1/2 to 3/4 inch thick. Arrange a bowl of salsa
or guacamole in the center of a serving platter. Surround
with the pinwheels cut side up. Serve the pinwheels with
the salsa or guacamole.

Yield: 60 servings

Hot Chile Quesadillas

12 flour tortillas
2 cups shredded longhorn, Monterey Jack or asadero
   cheese
2 (4-ounce) cans chopped green chiles, drained
Cumin to taste

Arrange 1 tortilla in a hot skillet sprayed with nonstick cooking
spray. Sprinkle with cheese, green chiles and a dash of cumin.
Moisten another tortilla with nonstick cooking spray or water.
Arrange over the top. Cook until brown on each side, turning
once. Remove to a warm 200-degree oven until ready to
serve. Repeat the process with the remaining ingredients. To
serve, cut the quesadillas into quarters using scissors. Serve
with salsa and/or sour cream.

Yield: 24 pieces

*Note: You may add cooked black beans, corn or shredded
cooked chicken.*

*After the guacamole
is made, put the
avocado seed back
in the mixture and
cover with plastic
wrap. Store in an
airtight container.
The dip will retain
its fresh green color.*

Bleu Cheese and Roasted Walnuts

1 cup walnut pieces
1 pound bleu cheese
1/4 cup (about) milk
Freshly ground white pepper
2 tablespoons olive oil
1 cup thinly sliced onions
1 cup julienned Granny Smith apple
Rice wine vinegar to taste
24 small rounds French bread, toasted

Spread the walnut pieces on a baking sheet. Bake at 350 degrees until toasted. Watch carefully to prevent burning. Crumble the bleu cheese in a food processor. Add the milk a small amount at a time, processing constantly until of the desired consistency. Add the toasted walnuts. Process until the walnuts are in small pieces but not pulverized. Stir in the white pepper.

Heat the olive oil in a sauté pan. Add the onions and apple. Sauté for 6 to 8 minutes or until caramelized. Remove from the heat. Stir in the rice wine vinegar. Let stand until cool. Spread a heaping spoonful of the cheese mixture on the French bread rounds. Top each with the apple onion mixture. Arrange on a serving platter.

Yield: 24 servings

Always roast or toast nuts before using them in a recipe. Run them in a hot oven on a baking sheet for just a minute or two. It's not necessary to add oil. The texture is improved and the flavor is intensified.

Hot and Sweet Pecans

1/2 cup chili oil
2 tablespoons chili powder
1/4 teaspoon cumin
1 teaspoon salt
3 tablespoons honey
4 cups pecan halves
Salt to taste

Heat the chili oil, chili powder, cumin, 1 teaspoon salt and honey in a skillet, stirring constantly. Remove from the heat. Add the pecan halves and stir to coat. Arrange in a single layer on a baking sheet. Bake at 350 degrees for 10 to 15 minutes or until crisp, stirring and shaking frequently to prevent overbrowning. Season with salt to taste.

Yield: 4 cups

Almond Tea

5 regular-size tea bags
3 cups boiling water
3/4 cup sugar
1/2 cup lemon juice
1/2 teaspoon almond extract
1 teaspoon vanilla extract

Steep the tea bags in boiling water in a small pitcher. Discard the tea bags. Add the sugar, lemon juice, almond extract and vanilla and mix well. Pour into a 1/2-gallon pitcher. Add enough water and ice cubes to fill the pitcher and mix well.

Yield: 8 (1-cup) servings

In a small ring mold arrange galax leaves and cranberries (use a lot of both). Fill the ring with water to the brim. Freeze. Unmold the ice at party time. Set a frozen bottle of the best vodka in the middle of the ring in the center of a rimmed silver tray. Serve the vodka in very small frozen glasses.

For a summer party, place violets, apple blossoms, or curls of lemon peel or small wedges of lime or slices of strawberry in ice trays before filling and freezing. Especially pretty in a clear drink like lemonade or ginger ale or vodka.

Spicy Iced Tea

1/4 cup artificial sweetener, or 2 cups sugar
4 cups water
10 large sprigs of fresh mint
2 family-size tea bags
2 Constant Comment tea bags
4 cups water

Bring the artificial sweetener and 4 cups water to a boil in a saucepan. Boil for 5 minutes. Remove from the heat. Add the mint sprigs and mash well. Add the tea bags and steep. Discard the tea bags. Let stand, covered, until cool. Remove the mint sprigs and discard. Add 4 cups water and mix well. Serve over ice in serving glasses.

Yield: 8 servings

Greensands, a Caribbean drink, is very refreshing after a long hike. Into a tall glass filled with ice cubes pour fresh lemonade and a cold beer. Try it; you'll love it.

In medieval times mint was thought to symbolize wisdom and virtue. And you can't make a mint julep without it. The newest flavor is chocolate mint. Toss the leaves with melon balls for a lovely cool dessert.

Swedish Glögg

3 cinnamon sticks
10 whole cloves
6 cardamom seeds
1 bottle domestic brandy
1 glass (or more) red wine
1 cup sugar
1/3 cup raisins
Blanched almonds
Fruit peel

Heat the cinnamon sticks, cloves and cardamom seeds in the brandy and wine in a saucepan. Cook gently for 15 minutes. Strain into a sterilized bottle, discarding the solids; seal tightly. Make the glögg a few days before serving.

To serve, reheat the glögg in a saucepan; do not boil. Sprinkle a few raisins, a few blanched almonds and bits of fruit peel in each serving cup. Add the hot glögg.

Yield: 6 servings

Soups, Salads & Vegetables

Select peaches with a creamy to gold under-color. The amount of red blush on the fruit depends on the variety and is not always a sign of ripeness. Two other indicators of ripeness are a well-defined crease and a good fragrance.

Fully ripened peaches should be immediately placed in the refrigerator and kept there until used. Sound and mature, but not overripe, peaches can be expected to hold for one to two weeks at 32 to 35 degrees.

There is no gain in sugar content once a peach is picked. Its ripening process consists primarily of softening and developing juice and flavor. So, the riper a peach is at harvest, the more sugar it contains.

Chilled Peach Soup

1 cup water
1/2 cup sugar
3/4 cup peach schnapps
3 pounds peaches, peeled, sliced
1/2 cup heavy cream
1 cup crème fraîche
1 tablespoon chopped tarragon or mint

Bring the water, sugar and schnapps to a boil in a saucepan. Boil until the sugar dissolves. Add the peaches. Return to a boil. Remove from the heat. Purée the peach mixture in batches in a food processor, pouring each batch into a large bowl after processing. Stir in the heavy cream. Chill, covered, in the refrigerator for up to 3 days. To serve, ladle the chilled soup into chilled soup bowls. Top with the crème fraîche and tarragon or mint.

Yield: 6 servings

Thai Ginger Soup

2 (15-ounce) cans coconut milk
2 to 4 tablespoons Thai fish sauce
2 to 4 tablespoons fresh lemon juice
1 (1/2- to 1-inch) piece gingerroot, cut into slivers
8 to 12 ounces shredded cooked chicken

Combine the coconut milk, fish sauce, lemon juice, gingerroot and chicken in a saucepan. Bring to a boil. Reduce the heat. Simmer for 5 to 30 minutes. Ladle into soup bowls. Garnish with finely sliced scallions and fresh cilantro.

Yield: 4 to 6 servings

Chicken Tortilla Soup

1 large onion, chopped
2 tablespoons vegetable oil
2 teaspoons chopped
  garlic
1 (4-ounce) can chopped
  green chiles
1 (15-ounce) can Italian
  stewed tomatoes
4 (14-ounce) cans chicken
  broth
1 tablespoon lemon pepper
2 tablespoons
  Worcestershire sauce

1 tablespoon chili powder
1 teaspoon cumin
1 teaspoon hot sauce
1/4 cup all-purpose flour
1/2 cup water
1 pound bone-in chicken
  breast, cooked, cubed
1/4 cup sour cream
  (optional)
Tortilla chips

Sauté the onion in the hot oil in a large saucepan until wilted.
Add the garlic. Cook for 1 minute. Add the green chiles,
tomatoes, chicken broth, lemon pepper, Worcestershire sauce,
chili powder, cumin and hot sauce and mix well. Cook for
20 minutes. Combine the flour and water in a bowl and whisk
well. Add to the soup gradually, stirring constantly. Boil for
5 minutes. Stir in the chicken and sour cream. Ladle into soup
bowls and serve with tortilla chips.

Yield: 8 servings

Traveling Soup

This soup is great to carry to a picnic.

2 chicken bouillon cubes
1 cup boiling water
1 (10-ounce) can cream of
  celery soup
1 cup sour cream

1 tablespoon chopped
  green bell pepper
1 tablespoon chopped
  green onions

Dissolve the bouillon cubes in the boiling water in a small
heatproof bowl. Combine the soup and sour cream in a bowl
and mix well. Add the bouillon and mix well. Stir in the bell
pepper and green onions. Chill, covered, for 8 to 12 hours. To
serve, ladle into soup bowls and garnish with paprika or sour
cream topped with caviar.

Yield: 8 servings

*It's TUESDAY. Do
you wonder why
the lines are so
long at Mountain
Fresh? It's vegetable
soup and corn
bread day.*

Bleu Cheese Tomato Soup

3 pounds ripe tomatoes, peeled, quartered, seeded
2 garlic cloves, minced
Salt and freshly ground pepper to taste
1 onion, chopped
2 ribs celery, chopped
1 carrot, chopped
2 tablespoons margarine
1 1/4 quarts unsalted chicken stock
4 ounces bleu cheese, crumbled
3 tablespoons heavy cream
6 basil leaves
1 cup crumbled cooked bacon
Chopped fresh basil

Spread the tomatoes in a shallow baking dish. Sprinkle with the garlic, salt and pepper. Bake at 400 degrees for 35 minutes or until roasted. Sauté the onion, celery and carrot in the margarine in a large saucepan. Sprinkle with salt and pepper. Cook over low heat for 10 minutes or until soft, stirring frequently. Stir in the chicken stock and roasted tomatoes. Bring to a boil and reduce the heat. Simmer, covered, for 20 minutes. Add the bleu cheese, cream and basil leaves. Process in batches in a food processor or blender just until blended. Return to the saucepan and adjust the seasonings. Reheat the soup but do not boil. Ladle into soup bowls. Sprinkle with the bacon and chopped fresh basil.

Yield: 4 servings

Food needs variety of textures as well as variety of flavors, especially in dips, soups, and spreads. Avoid the overly processed puréed consistency (unless, of course, that is what you're after) by adding portions of ingredients at different times during the blending. You'll end up with varied sizes of chunks and pieces and of smoothness.

Southwestern Soup

1 tablespoon vegetable oil
2 cups minced red onion
1/3 cup uncooked rice
3 (14-ounce) cans chicken broth
1/2 cup (or more) water
2 (14-ounce) cans black beans, drained, rinsed
1 (10-ounce) package frozen Shoe Peg corn
3/4 teaspoon cumin
4 cups fresh spinach leaves
1/2 cup cilantro leaves
1/2 cup salsa
Salt and pepper to taste
3/4 cup shredded sharp Cheddar cheese

Heat the oil in a large stockpot. Add the onion and uncooked rice. Sauté for 4 minutes or until the rice is brown. Add the chicken broth, water, black beans, corn and cumin. Bring to a boil and reduce the heat. Simmer, covered, for 15 to 18 minutes or until the rice is tender. Cut the spinach leaves into wide strips. Add the spinach, cilantro and salsa and mix well. Adjust the liquid as needed. Season with salt and pepper. Ladle into soup bowls. Sprinkle with the Cheddar cheese.

Yield: 8 servings

Mustard Coleslaw

3 1/2 cups finely chopped cabbage	3 tablespoons vegetable oil
1 small green bell pepper, chopped	3 tablespoons lemon juice
1/4 cup chopped celery	1 1/2 tablespoons prepared mustard
1/4 cup chopped parsley	1 tablespoon sugar
1 medium onion, chopped	1 teaspoon salt
	1/2 teaspoon celery seeds

Combine the cabbage, bell pepper, celery, parsley and onion in a large bowl and toss to mix. Combine the oil, lemon juice, mustard, sugar, salt and celery seeds in a bowl and whisk well. Pour over the cabbage mixture and toss to coat. Pack into a salad mold. Chill, covered, in the refrigerator until ready to serve. Unmold onto a serving plate.

Yield: 4 to 6 servings

Get in the habit of making your own chicken stock once a month or so and storing it in one-cup containers in the freezer. Your friends will think you've gone to cooking school.

Almond and Orange Salad

1/4 cup sliced almonds	Dash of pepper
4 teaspoons sugar	Dash of Tabasco sauce
1/4 cup salad oil	1 head romaine, torn into
2 tablespoons vinegar	bite-size pieces
2 tablespoons sugar	1 cup chopped celery
1 tablespoon snipped fresh	2 scallions, chopped
parsley	1 (11-ounce) can mandarin
1/2 teaspoon salt	oranges, drained

Sauté the almonds in 4 teaspoons sugar in a skillet over
low heat until the sugar melts and coats the almonds.
Combine the salad oil, vinegar, 2 tablespoons sugar, parsley,
salt, pepper and Tabasco sauce in a bowl and whisk well.
Combine the romaine, celery and scallions in a large bowl.
Add the mandarin oranges and almonds and toss to mix.
Drizzle with the dressing and toss to coat. Serve immediately.

Yield: 6 servings

Smoked Salmon on Salad Greens

1/4 cup olive oil	8 ounces Norwegian
1 tablespoon red wine	smoked salmon,
vinegar	thinly sliced
1 tablespoon chopped	1 red onion, thinly sliced
fresh chives	8 teaspoons drained capers
Freshly ground pepper	Freshly grated Parmesan
to taste	cheese to taste
Mixed salad greens for 8	

Combine the olive oil, red wine vinegar, chives and pepper in
a jar with a tight-fitting lid. Cover with the lid and shake to
mix well. Adjust the seasonings to taste. Drizzle over the mixed
salad greens in a large salad bowl and toss to coat. Divide the
salad among 8 salad plates. Top with the salmon, red onion
and capers. Sprinkle with Parmesan cheese.

Yield: 8 servings

Dandelions can be a pest in a lovely green lawn, but they are used in many cultures in different ways. Young greens are good boiled with salt and olive oil, added to salads, or chopped up in scrambled eggs. Wine is made from the flowers, and the roots are roasted and used as a drink like coffee.

Poached Salmon and Pasta with Cucumber Dressing

Favorite poaching broth
2 pounds fresh salmon fillets
8 ounces spinach fettuccini, cooked
8 ounces yellow fettuccini, cooked
1 tablespoon olive oil
1 or 2 heads Boston leaf lettuce
Cucumber Dressing (below)

Bring your favorite poaching broth to a boil in a large saucepan. Add the salmon and reduce the heat to a simmer. Poach for 10 to 12 minutes or until the salmon flakes easily with a fork. Lift from the broth and place on a plate. Let stand until cool. Cut into bite-size pieces. Drain the spinach fettuccini and yellow fettuccini. Place in a large bowl. Drizzle with the olive oil and toss to coat. Let stand until cool.

To serve, arrange a nest of the mixed pasta on a leaf of Boston lettuce on each serving plate. Top with the salmon. Spoon the Cucumber Dressing over the salmon.

Yield: 6 to 8 servings

Cucumber Dressing

1 cup sour cream
2 tablespoons white vinegar
2 cucumbers, seeded, chopped
1 tablespoon fresh dill
1/2 teaspoon salt
1/2 teaspoon white pepper

Combine the sour cream, vinegar, cucumbers, dill, salt and white pepper in a bowl and mix well.

The Hillbilly Day Parades of the early fifties challenged everyone's creativity. Young Tudor (Buddy) Hall's hand-fashioned outhouse perched loftily on top of his 1928 Ford was the most memorable sight.

Southwestern Bean Salad

2 avocados, peeled, cut into 1/2-inch pieces
Lemon juice
1 cup frozen whole kernel corn
6 cups cooked black beans
1 tomato, chopped
1 red bell pepper, chopped
1 small red onion, chopped
1/2 jalapeño, seeded, minced
1/3 cup olive oil
2 tablespoons white wine vinegar
1/4 cup chopped cilantro
Salt and pepper to taste

Toss the avocado pieces in lemon juice in a small bowl to prevent darkening. Pour boiling water over the corn in a heatproof bowl. Let stand for 15 minutes; drain. Combine the avocado pieces, corn, black beans, tomato, bell pepper, red onion, chile, olive oil, white wine vinegar, cilantro, salt and pepper in a large bowl and mix well. Chill, covered, for 2 hours or longer before serving.

Yield: 6 to 8 servings

Note: You may use rinsed, drained canned black beans.

Tomato Cucumber Platter with Feta

1/2 cup olive oil
1/2 cup balsamic vinegar
1 teaspoon dry mustard
Salt and pepper to taste
5 large ripe tomatoes, sliced
5 cucumbers, sliced
4 ounces feta cheese, crumbled
Torn fresh basil or thyme to taste

Combine the olive oil, balsamic vinegar, dry mustard, salt and pepper in a jar with a tight-fitting lid. Cover with the lid and shake well. Arrange the tomatoes and cucumbers on a serving platter. Sprinkle with the feta cheese and basil. Drizzle with some of the vinaigrette and serve with the remaining vinaigrette.

Yield: 8 to 10 servings

Note: Do not use dried herbs in this recipe.

Cucumber Ring

2 cups grated seeded peeled cucumbers
1/2 teaspoon salt
1/8 teaspoon white pepper
2 cups sour cream
2 tablespoons cider vinegar
2 tablespoons lemon juice
3 tablespoons chopped pimentos
1 tablespoon chopped chives
2 tablespoons unflavored gelatin
1/2 cup cold water

Season the cucumbers with salt and white pepper in a bowl. Mix the sour cream, vinegar, lemon juice, pimentos and chives in a large bowl. Sprinkle the gelatin over the cold water in a double boiler. Let stand for 5 minutes. Heat over hot water until dissolved. Add to the sour cream mixture and mix well. Stir in the cucumbers. Pour into a lightly oiled 5-cup ring mold. Chill for 4 hours. Unmold onto a serving platter. Fill the center as desired. Garnish with watercress.

Yield: 10 servings

Spicy Tomato Aspic

4 cups chilled spicy vegetable juice cocktail
2 (3-ounce) packages lemon gelatin
1 teaspoon onion salt
1 teaspoon Worcestershire sauce
Chopped celery, chopped green bell pepper, sliced olives
    or shrimp (optional)

Bring 2 cups of the vegetable juice cocktail to a boil in a saucepan. Add the gelatin. Heat until dissolved, stirring constantly. Remove from the heat. Add the remaining 2 cups cold vegetable juice cocktail, onion salt and Worcestershire sauce and mix well. Stir in the celery, bell pepper, olives or shrimp. Pour into a mold. Chill until firm.

Yield: 8 servings

Note: You may make the aspic less spicy by using 2 cups spicy vegetable juice cocktail and 2 cups regular vegetable juice cocktail.

Chives make lovely little touches of green in the garden. They can be cut as needed without disturbing the plant's symmetry. The blooms are ornamental and later give bounteous seeds.

Rainbow Pasta Salad

12 ounces rainbow rotini, cooked al dente, drained
Florets of 1 small bunch broccoli
3 green onions, chopped
1 rib celery, chopped
1 (4-ounce) can pitted black olives, drained
1/4 cup stuffed green olives
1 (14-ounce) can artichokes, drained
1/2 green bell pepper, coarsely chopped
1/2 red bell pepper, coarsely chopped
1/2 yellow bell pepper, coarsely chopped
3/4 tablespoon garlic salt
3/4 tablespoon parsley
3/4 tablespoon seasoned salt
Salt and pepper to taste
1/4 cup freshly grated Parmesan cheese
1/2 cup olive oil
3 tablespoons apple cider vinegar

Combine the pasta, broccoli, green onions, celery, black olives, green olives, artichokes and bell peppers in a large bowl and toss to mix. Season with the garlic salt, parsley, seasoned salt, salt and pepper. Sprinkle with the Parmesan cheese. Add the olive oil and apple cider vinegar and toss to mix well. Chill, covered, for 24 hours.

Yield: 8 to 10 servings

Curried Rice Salad

2 cups uncooked rice
6 bouillon cubes
1 (6-ounce) jar marinated artichoke hearts
1/2 cup mayonnaise
1 teaspoon curry powder
6 green onions, sliced
1/2 green bell pepper, chopped
12 stuffed olives, chopped

Cook the rice using the package directions and adding 6 bouillon cubes. Drain the artichoke hearts, reserving the marinade. Chop the artichoke hearts. Mix the reserved marinade, mayonnaise and curry powder in a bowl. Combine the rice, artichoke hearts, green onions, bell pepper and olives in a large bowl and mix well. Add the mayonnaise mixture and mix well. Chill, covered, until ready to serve. Toss before serving.

Yield: 6 servings

Roasted Sesame Asparagus

6 asparagus spears
Olive oil
Salt and pepper to taste
Untoasted sesame seeds

Arrange the asparagus in uniform direction in a glass baking dish sprayed with nonstick cooking spray. Pour olive oil over the asparagus to lightly coat. Sprinkle with salt, pepper and sesame seeds. Bake at 425 degrees for 15 minutes. Do not overcook; the asparagus will continue to cook after removal from the oven. Serve hot, at room temperature or chilled.

Yield: 1 serving

Steamed Asparagus with Lemon Garlic Vinaigrette

1 pound asparagus, rinsed, trimmed
2 small garlic cloves
3/4 cup olive oil
1/2 teaspoon coarse salt
2 teaspoons Dijon mustard
1/2 teaspoon sugar
3 tablespoons lemon juice

Steam the asparagus for 3 to 5 minutes or until tender-crisp; drain. Place in a bowl of ice water. Let stand until cool. Drain and pat dry. Chill, covered, until serving time. Arrange on a serving plate. Process the garlic, olive oil, salt, mustard, sugar and lemon juice in a blender until smooth. Drizzle over the asparagus.

Yield: 6 servings

Many people share Edith Inglesby's feelings about the return to Highlands each summer. "We had, oh blessed thought, arrived in Highlands! The long summer stretched before me in a haze of delights. Such was my content that subconsciously I was thinking: nothing can ever go wrong. We are in Highlands!"

Broccoli with Ripe Olive Sauce

2 garlic cloves, crushed
1/2 cup olive oil
1/2 cup minced ripe olives
1 to 2 teaspoons lemon juice
Salt and freshly ground pepper to taste
1 bunch broccoli

Sauté the garlic in the olive oil in a small saucepan over medium-low heat until light golden brown; do not brown. Remove the garlic and discard. Add the olives, lemon juice and a generous amount of salt and pepper to the saucepan. Sauté for 1 to 2 minutes. Turn off the heat.

Trim the large stems from the broccoli. Divide the broccoli into florets. Steam the broccoli in a steamer until tender-crisp. Reheat the olive sauce until sizzling. Arrange the broccoli on serving plates. Pour the hot olive sauce over the top.

Yield: 4 servings

Pineapple Carrots

10 medium carrots, diagonally sliced
1 (15-ounce) can pineapple tidbits
1 cup orange juice
1 tablespoon cornstarch
1 teaspoon salt
1/2 teaspoon cinnamon

Cook the carrots in boiling water to cover in a saucepan for 10 minutes or until tender; drain. Drain the pineapple, reserving the juice. Combine the reserved pineapple juice, orange juice, cornstarch, salt and cinnamon in a medium saucepan and blend well. Cook over medium heat until thickened and smooth, stirring constantly. Add the carrots and pineapple. Cook until heated through, stirring constantly.

Yield: 8 servings

Corn, Black Bean and Tomato Skillet

1 (12- to 18-ounce) package frozen Shoe Peg corn
2 tablespoons olive oil
2 (14-ounce) cans black beans, rinsed, drained
1 (14-ounce) can diced tomatoes
1 teaspoon jalapeño juice, or $1/2$ fresh jalapeño, seeded, chopped
$3/4$ teaspoon cumin
Salt and pepper to taste
Chopped fresh cilantro

Sauté the frozen corn in the olive oil in a skillet for a few minutes. Add the black beans and undrained tomatoes and mix well. Stir in the jalapeño juice, cumin, salt and pepper. Cook until heated through. Sprinkle with cilantro.

Yield: 8 servings

Haricots Verts with Parsley and Lemon Juice

4 quarts water
Salt to taste
$11/2$ pounds fresh green beans, trimmed, French cut (haricots verts)
$1/4$ cup ($1/2$ stick) butter
$1/4$ cup pine nuts
5 to 6 tablespoons minced parsley
Juice of 1 to 2 lemons
Pepper to taste
Sprigs of fresh parsley

Bring the water to a boil in a 5- or 6-quart saucepan. Season lightly with salt. Add the green beans. Cook for 5 minutes; drain. Plunge immediately into cold water to stop the cooking process.

Melt the butter in a large heavy skillet. Add the pine nuts. Sauté until lightly toasted. Add the green beans and toss to coat. Add 5 to 6 tablespoons parsley and lemon juice. Sauté until all of the ingredients are combined. Season with salt and pepper. Garnish with sprigs of fresh parsley.

Yield: 6 to 8 servings

A visitor to Highlands in 1898, Bradford Torrey, enjoyed what many Highlanders today enjoy. "What could a man want better than a long unhurried day on those romantic mountain roads, with birds singing from every bush and new and lovely flowers inviting his hand at every turn? With fair weather and in a fair country, walking is its own reward." On a walk to Turtle Pond he reports: "I recall especially great numbers of tiny yellow lady's slipper and beds of white flowered clintonia, the latter a novelty to me. Along the brookside grew splendid Halesia trees, full of white bells and the more splendid crab-apple tree, one of the glories of America."

Portobello Mushroom Stacks

1 eggplant
1 large zucchini
1 large yellow squash
12 portobello mushroom caps
Olive oil or vinaigrette salad dressing
2 large red bell peppers, cut into thirds, seeded, roasted, peeled
4 ounces (about) goat cheese
4 or 5 large fresh basil leaves

Cut the eggplant, zucchini and yellow squash into 8 thin slices. Remove any stems from the mushrooms. Coat the vegetable slices and mushrooms lightly with olive oil. Arrange on a vegetable grill rack. Grill over low heat until tender. To create one stack, place a mushroom cap gill side down. Layer 1 slice bell pepper, 1 slice zucchini, 1 slice yellow squash and 1 slice eggplant on the mushroom cap. Top with another mushroom cap gill side down. Repeat the vegetable layers. Spread 1 to 2 teaspoons of the goat cheese on the slice of eggplant. Add 1 large basil leaf and another mushroom cap. Place the stack on a baking sheet lined with parchment paper. Repeat the layering for 3 more stacks. Bake at 350 degrees for 5 minutes.

Yield: 4 servings

Colcannon (Cabbage and Potatoes)

1¹/₂ pounds potatoes
¹/₂ teaspoon salt
1¹/₂ cups chopped green cabbage
¹/₃ cup finely chopped green onions
2 cups boiling water
²/₃ cup milk
2 tablespoons butter or margarine
¹/₂ teaspoon salt
¹/₈ teaspoon freshly ground pepper

Peel the potatoes. Cut into 2-inch pieces and place in a large saucepan. Add enough cold water to cover the potatoes by 2 inches. Sprinkle with ¹/₂ teaspoon salt. Bring to a boil. Boil for 5 minutes. Add the cabbage. Boil for 10 minutes longer or until the potatoes are tender.

Place the green onions in a sieve. Pour the boiling water over the green onions; drain. Combine the green onions, milk, butter, ¹/₂ teaspoon salt and pepper in a medium saucepan. Bring to a boil. Remove from the heat.

Drain the potatoes and cabbage. Beat at low speed until coarsely mashed. Add the green onion mixture gradually, beating at high speed. Continue to beat until the potatoes are light and fluffy.

Yield: 4 cups

Three things you need to know about potatoes:

• The brown rough-skinned russets (mainly from Idaho) are best for baking, mashing, and French frying. Russets have a high starch content that makes them fluffy.

• Waxy potatoes, with more moisture and a low starch content, like the Red Bliss, are better for oven roasting. The russet is just too dry to roast properly.

• New potatoes and medium-starch potatoes like the Yukon Gold have a high moisture content and hold their shape while boiling, steaming, or pan roasting.

A single potato
can supply half a
day's requirement
for vitamin C.

The Inca Indians
of Peru began
cultivating the
potato about two
hundred years
before the birth
of Christ. Spanish
soldiers discovered
the tubers growing
in the Andes in 1537
and took them
home to Europe.

Whipped Potatoes with Garlic and Chives

4 cups cubed peeled baking potatoes
  (about 1 1/2 pounds)
2 teaspoons minced garlic
2 tablespoons chopped fresh chives
3/4 cup low-fat milk
3 tablespoons grated Parmesan cheese
1 tablespoon butter or margarine
Salt and pepper to taste

Place the potatoes in a medium saucepan and add enough water to cover. Bring to a boil and reduce the heat. Simmer, covered, for 15 to 17 minutes or until the potatoes are tender; drain. Process the potatoes, garlic, chives, milk, Parmesan cheese, butter, salt and pepper in a food processor until smooth. Adjust the seasonings to taste. Spoon onto serving plates.

Yield: 4 servings

Note: You may spoon into a pastry bag and pipe as desired on serving plates.

Herb Baked Tomatoes

6 large ripe fresh tomatoes
6 teaspoons olive oil
Salt and pepper to taste
3 garlic cloves, minced
3 tablespoons chopped fresh basil

Cut the tomatoes into halves horizontally. Arrange the tomatoes cut side up on a baking sheet. Drizzle with the olive oil. Sprinkle with salt and pepper. Bake at 325 degrees for 1 to 1 1/2 hours. Sprinkle with the garlic. Bake for 1 to 1 1/2 hours longer or until the tomatoes collapse and begin to caramelize. Sprinkle with the basil just before serving. Serve hot or at room temperature.

Yield: 6 servings

Highlands Tomato Pie

1 cup mayonnaise
1 cup shredded sharp Cheddar cheese
1 teaspoon garlic salt or garlic powder
1 teaspoon ground pepper
1 teaspoon chopped chives
1 teaspoon chopped basil
1 teaspoon onion powder or flakes
3 large tomatoes, thickly sliced
1 baked (9-inch) pie shell

Combine the mayonnaise, Cheddar cheese, garlic salt, pepper, chives, basil and onion powder in a bowl and mix well. Arrange the tomatoes in the baked pie shell. Spoon the Cheddar cheese mixture over the top and press down. Bake at 400 degrees for 40 to 45 minutes or until heated through. Cool slightly before cutting. Serve hot or cold.

Yield: 6 to 8 servings

Note: You may use 6 Roma tomatoes instead of the large tomatoes.

The Cherokee name for Highlands is Onteeorah. It means "hills of the sky."

Satulah *means "puff of wind."*

Unaka Kanoos *is "white mountain" or "Whiteside Mountain."*

Cullasaja *is "sweet water."*

Wayah *is "wolf."*

Ellijay *is "verdant earth."*

Tomatoes Stuffed with Squash

1 pound yellow squash, trimmed, grated
1 pound zucchini, trimmed, grated
2 teaspoons salt
8 small tomatoes
Salt and pepper to taste
Vegetable oil
1 onion, minced
1 garlic clove, minced
2 tablespoons olive oil
2 tablespoons butter
1 cup heavy cream
1/2 cup grated Gruyère cheese
1/4 cup grated Parmesan cheese

Place the squash and zucchini in a colander. Sprinkle with 2 teaspoons salt and toss to mix. Drain for 30 minutes. Place the squash mixture in a clean tea towel and squeeze out the excess moisture.

Cut a 3/4-inch slice from the top of each of the tomatoes. Remove the seeds and juice with a demitasse spoon without squeezing the tomatoes. Sprinkle with salt and pepper to taste. Brush with vegetable oil. Arrange the tomatoes cut side up on a baking sheet. Bake at 350 degrees for 10 minutes. Invert onto a wire rack and let drain for 30 minutes.

Sauté the onion and garlic in the olive oil and butter until the onion is tender. Stir in the squash mixture. Cook for 2 minutes. Add the cream. Cook until the cream is absorbed. Remove from the heat. Stir in the Gruyère cheese and Parmesan cheese. Spoon into the tomatoes. Arrange on a baking sheet. Broil for 4 minutes. Serve immediately.

Yield: 8 servings

The first zucchini I ever saw I killed it with a hoe.
—*John Gould,*
Monstrous Depravity, *1963*

Squash Gratin with White Cheddar Cheese

1 medium onion, thinly sliced
2 pounds yellow squash, thinly sliced
1 teaspoon salt
Freshly ground pepper to taste
2 eggs
2 tablespoons sugar
1/2 cup milk
8 ounces Vermont or New York white Cheddar cheese,
   shredded
1 to 2 tablespoons butter

Bring enough water to cover the onion and squash to a boil in a saucepan. Add the onion and squash. Cook for 10 to 15 minutes or until tender; drain. Arrange in a 2-quart baking dish. Sprinkle with the salt and pepper. Combine the eggs, sugar, milk and cheese in a bowl and mix well. Pour over the squash mixture. Dot with thin slices of butter. Bake at 350 degrees for 45 minutes. Cut into squares or diamond shapes.

Yield: 6 to 8 servings

Oven-Roasted Root Vegetables

3 tablespoons olive oil
12 new potatoes, cut into halves
4 sweet potatoes, peeled, cut into 3-inch pieces
8 carrots, cut into 3-inch pieces
6 parsnips, cut into 3-inch pieces
1 tablespoon salt

Pour the olive oil into a large baking pan. Add the potatoes, sweet potatoes, carrots and parsnips and stir to coat. Sprinkle with the salt. Bake at 375 degrees for 30 to 40 minutes or until tender, turning once or twice to prevent sticking.

Note: You may use any combination of vegetables, including onions, eggplant, zucchini, yellow squash and tomatoes. If the parsnips are large, blanch them in boiling water for 5 minutes before roasting.

Yield: 6 to 8 servings

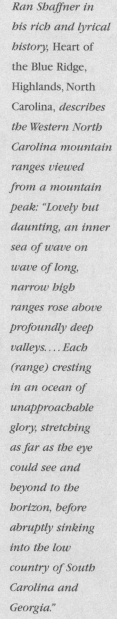

Ran Shaffner in his rich and lyrical history, Heart of the Blue Ridge, Highlands, North Carolina, *describes the Western North Carolina mountain ranges viewed from a mountain peak: "Lovely but daunting, an inner sea of wave on wave of long, narrow high ranges rose above profoundly deep valleys. . . . Each (range) cresting in an ocean of unapproachable glory, stretching as far as the eye could see and beyond to the horizon, before abruptly sinking into the low country of South Carolina and Georgia."*

Matchstick Vegetables with Lemon Thyme Butter

1¹/2 ounces carrots
1¹/2 ounces squash
1¹/2 ounces red cabbage
1¹/2 ounces snow peas
1¹/2 ounces leeks
1¹/2 ounces shiitake mushrooms
1¹/2 ounces celery
¹/4 cup olive oil
Pinch of salt and white pepper
Lemon Thyme Butter (below)

Cut the carrots, squash, red cabbage, snow peas, leeks, shiitake mushrooms and celery into very thin strips. Heat the olive oil in a large sauté pan. Add the vegetables. Sauté for 1¹/2 minutes or until the colors of the vegetables intensify. Season with salt and white pepper. Serve immediately with Lemon Thyme Butter.

Yield: 6 servings

Lemon Thyme Butter

1 tablespoon butter, softened
¹/2 teaspoon lemon juice
¹/2 teaspoon finely minced parsley
1¹/2 teaspoons finely minced lemon thyme

Combine the butter, lemon juice, parsley and thyme in a bowl and mix well.

Onions, garlic, and asparagus are lilies; the sweet potato is a morning glory; and peanuts are beans, not nuts. Got all that?

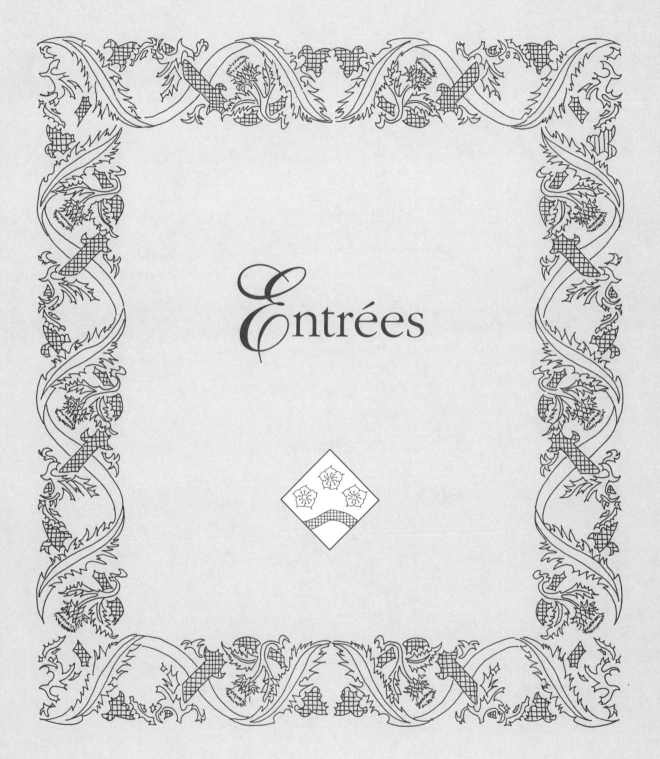

Entrées

If you dine under an umbrella in summertime, create a bit of magic by stringing twinkly lights around the pole and through the spokes of the umbrella. You'll have a canopy of fireflies.

For a casual buffet centerpiece, arrange colorful six-packs of annuals and pretty new gardening gloves and a bright red trowel.

For a supper after a musical event, use a musical instrument for the centerpiece, some sheet music, a loose bouquet, and a long ribbon to wind through the instrument and the sheets of music.

Grilled Flank Steak with Black Bean and Corn Salsa

1 pound flank steak
1/2 cup dry red wine
3 garlic cloves, pressed
2 tablespoons chopped shallots
2 tablespoons Worcestershire sauce
1/4 cup lemon juice
1 1/2 teaspoons pepper
1/2 teaspoon garlic powder
Black Bean and Corn Salsa (below)
1/2 avocado, sliced

Place the steak in a sealable plastic food storage bag. Combine the wine, garlic, shallots, Worcestershire sauce, lemon juice, pepper and garlic powder in a bowl and mix well. Pour over the steak and seal the bag. Marinate in the refrigerator for 8 to 12 hours, turning occasionally; drain. Place the steak on a grill rack. Grill for 7 minutes on each side or until of the desired degree of doneness. Cut the steak diagonally into slices. Serve with Black Bean and Corn Salsa and avocado slices.

Yield: 2 servings

Black Bean and Corn Salsa

1 1/2 cups frozen whole kernel corn, thawed
1 (16-ounce) can black beans, rinsed, drained
1 jalapeño, seeded, finely chopped
1 garlic clove, pressed
2 tablespoons lime juice
2 tablespoons chopped fresh cilantro
1/4 teaspoon salt
1/4 teaspoon pepper

Combine the corn, black beans, chile, garlic, lime juice, cilantro, salt and pepper in a bowl and mix well.

New Orleans Veal Scallops

2 pounds round veal or scallopini
2 tablespoons all-purpose flour
Salt and pepper to taste
3 tablespoons butter
2 small onions, chopped
1 garlic clove, chopped
1 rib celery, chopped
1/2 green bell pepper, chopped
1 bay leaf
1/2 teaspoon thyme
1 teaspoon salt
1/4 teaspoon black pepper
Dash of cayenne pepper
2 cups beef broth
2 tablespoons tomato paste
Chopped fresh parsley

Cut the veal into slices about 1/2 to 3/4 inch thick. Season the flour with salt and pepper to taste on a nonbreakable surface. Add the veal. Pound in the seasoned flour. Sauté in the butter in a skillet over high heat until brown. Add the onions, garlic, celery, bell pepper, bay leaf, thyme, 1 teaspoon salt, 1/4 teaspoon black pepper and cayenne pepper. Cook until the vegetables are slightly limp. Mix the beef broth and tomato paste in a bowl. Add to the veal mixture. Cook, covered, over low heat for 35 to 45 minutes or until the veal is tender. Discard the bay leaf. Arrange the veal on a serving platter. Pour the sauce over the top. Sprinkle generously with parsley.

Yield: 6 to 8 servings

When cooking vegetables, particularly if caramelizing them, take out some pieces to add later for a variety of textures.

Lamb Shanks Deluxe

4 meaty lamb shanks
1/2 lemon
1/4 teaspoon garlic powder, or to taste
1 cup all-purpose flour
2 teaspoons salt
1 teaspoon pepper
1/2 cup olive oil
1 (10-ounce) can beef consommé
1 cup water
1/2 to 3/4 cup dry vermouth
1 medium onion, chopped
4 ribs celery, sliced
4 carrots, sliced

Rub the lamb with the lemon. Sprinkle with garlic powder. Let stand for 10 minutes. Combine the flour, salt and pepper in a nonrecycled paper bag and shake to mix well. Add 1 lamb shank and shake to coat. Remove to a plate. Repeat the process with the remaining lamb shanks. Reserve 1/4 cup of the flour mixture. Brown the lamb shanks in the olive oil in a skillet. Arrange in a single layer in a large baking dish. Add the reserved flour mixture to the pan drippings. Cook until brown, whisking constantly. Add the consommé, water and vermouth. Cook until slightly thickened, stirring constantly. Add the onion. Pour over the lamb shanks. You may chill the lamb shanks, covered, until ready to bake. Bake, uncovered, at 350 degrees for 1 1/2 hours. Turn the shanks. Add the celery and carrots. Bake for 1 hour longer.

Yield: 4 servings

To produce an even brown crust on food you are sautéing, have the food dry and at room temperature. Use a hard-anodized sauté pan (such as Calphalon). Heat the oil in the pan before adding food. Don't crowd the pieces together. Turn only once. A stainless steel pan produces less crust and a nonstick surface produces the least of all.

Cold Oriental Loin of Pork with Horseradish Applesauce

1 (5- to 6-pound) pork
    loin roast, boned, tied
Dry mustard to taste
Thyme to taste
1/2 cup sherry
1/2 cup soy sauce
3 garlic cloves, minced

2 tablespoons grated fresh
    gingerroot
1 (8-ounce) jar currant jelly
1 tablespoon soy sauce
2 tablespoons sherry
Horseradish Applesauce
    (below)

Rub the pork with dry mustard and thyme. Place in a sealable plastic food storage bag. Mix 1/2 cup sherry, 1/2 cup soy sauce, garlic and gingerroot in a bowl. Pour over the pork and seal the bag. Marinate in the refrigerator for 8 to 12 hours. Drain the pork, reserving the marinade. Boil the reserved marinade in a saucepan for 3 minutes, stirring constantly. Remove from the heat. Arrange the pork in a roasting pan. Bake at 325 degrees for 25 minutes per pound or until a meat thermometer inserted into the thickest portion registers 175 degrees, basting several times with the cooked marinade. Arrange the pork on a serving platter.

Melt the jelly in a heavy saucepan over medium heat. Add 1 tablespoon soy sauce and 2 tablespoons sherry and mix well. Cook for 1 to 2 minutes or until the mixture is reduced. Spoon over the pork and let stand until cool. Garnish with sliced tomatoes, thinly sliced red onion and sliced cucumbers. Serve at room temperature with Horseradish Applesauce.

Yield: 6 servings

Note: Do not allow the pork to stand at room temperature for more than 2 hours.

Horseradish Applesauce

1/4 cup prepared
    horseradish, or to taste

2 cups chunky applesauce

Combine the horseradish and applesauce in a bowl and blend well. Chill, covered, in the refrigerator until ready to serve.

At Halloween, Highlanders young and old dress up and head downtown to trick-or-treat the merchants. It's the biggest block party in the mountains. But if you stay at home, float something weird in your punch bowl, or maybe in the tub where your children bob for apples. Freeze water in disposable plastic gloves (don't use the ones with powder inside). Fill them with water, tie a knot, freeze them, then peel off the glove. A real attention getter in the punch bowl.

Garlic Cilantro Grilled Pork Tenderloin

2 pork tenderloins (about 1¹/2 pounds)
4 garlic cloves, minced
¹/4 cup olive oil
¹/2 cup chopped fresh cilantro
3 tablespoons fresh lime juice
Freshly ground pepper to taste

Place the pork in a sealable plastic food storage bag. Combine the garlic, olive oil, cilantro, lime juice and pepper in a bowl and mix well. Pour over the pork and seal the bag. Marinate for 4 to 12 hours. Drain the pork, discarding the marinade. Place the pork on a grill rack. Grill until a meat thermometer inserted into the thickest portion registers 155 degrees.

Note: You may slice the uncooked tenderloin into 1-inch pieces and flatten slightly before adding to the marinade. When ready to cook, arrange in a heavy skillet and pan-broil over medium-high heat for 2 to 3 minutes per side.

Yield: 6 servings

Roast Chicken

1 (4-pound) chicken
20 garlic cloves, peeled
1 teaspoon thyme
Salt and pepper to taste
4 oranges
¹/2 bottle red wine
¹/2 (8-ounce) jar red currant jelly
¹/2 cup chicken stock

Arrange the chicken on the garlic in a roasting pan. Rub with the thyme, salt and pepper. Remove the zest from 1 of the oranges. Coat the chicken with the zest. Squeeze the juice from the 4 oranges and pour over the chicken. Fill the chicken cavity with the squeezed oranges. Bake at 350 degrees for 2 hours. Remove the oranges. Place the chicken on a platter and tent with foil to keep warm. Skim most of the fat from the pan drippings. Add the wine, jelly and chicken stock to the drippings. Cook until thickened, stirring constantly. Serve the chicken with the sauce.

Yield: 4 servings

A three-pound rotisserie chicken yields a little less than two cups white meat and two cups dark. Chicken salad is a lot better when made with a roasted, rather than boiled, chicken.

For crisper skin on a roasted chicken, leave the bird uncovered in the refrigerator to dry out the skin the night before you intend to roast it.

Chicken Breast with Shrimp in Champagne Sauce

8 boneless skinless chicken breasts
Salt and pepper to taste
All-purpose flour for coating
2 tablespoons butter
12 ounces sliced fresh mushrooms
2 tablespoons butter
1 1/2 pounds uncooked shrimp, peeled, deveined
4 green onions, sliced
1 tablespoon lemon juice
2 tablespoons all-purpose flour
1 tablespoon chicken bouillon granules
1 teaspoon salt
3/4 cup water
1 1/2 cups half-and-half
3/4 cup (or more) Champagne

Season the chicken with salt and pepper to taste. Coat with some flour. Sauté the chicken in 2 tablespoons butter in a skillet until brown. Arrange in a baking dish. Bake at 250 degrees until cooked through.

Sauté the mushrooms in 2 tablespoons butter in a skillet until tender. Toss the uncooked shrimp, green onions and lemon juice in a bowl. Sauté the shrimp mixture in a large nonstick skillet over medium heat until the shrimp turn pink. Remove the shrimp to a warm platter, reserving the drippings in the skillet. Mix the flour, bouillon granules, 1 teaspoon salt and water in a small bowl. Add to the reserved drippings in the skillet gradually, stirring constantly. Add the half-and-half. Cook until thickened, stirring constantly. Stir in the sautéed mushrooms, shrimp and Champagne. Cook until heated through. Spoon over the chicken. Serve over hot cooked rice.

Yield: 8 servings

Everything that slows us down and forces patience, everything that sets us back into the slow cycles of nature is a help. Gardening is an instrument of grace.
—May Sarton, 1912

Exotic Chicken with Thai Sauce

8 boneless chicken breasts
1/2 (8-ounce) bottle South Seas salad dressing
Juice of 1/2 lemon
Freshly ground pepper to taste
1/2 cup (1 stick) butter, cut into pieces
2 tablespoons cornstarch
2 tablespoons cold water
6 garlic cloves, minced
2 tablespoons minced fresh gingerroot
1/2 cup minced green onions
1/2 cup minced fresh basil
1/4 cup minced fresh mint
2 cups unsweetened coconut milk
1/4 cup light soy sauce
1 teaspoon turmeric
1 teaspoon Chinese chili sauce, or to taste
1 teaspoon salt
Sprigs of fresh mint

Pound the chicken lightly to flatten and make a uniform size. Place in a sealable plastic food storage bag. Pour the salad dressing and lemon juice over the chicken and seal the bag. Marinate in the refrigerator for 1 hour or longer. Drain the chicken, discarding the marinade. Arrange the chicken in a roasting pan. Season with pepper and dot with the butter. Roast at 425 degrees for 30 to 40 minutes or until cooked through, basting every 10 minutes with the pan drippings. Remove the chicken to a warm platter. Reserve 1/4 cup of the pan drippings in the pan, discarding the remaining drippings.

Combine the cornstarch with the cold water in a small bowl and mix well. Combine the garlic, gingerroot, green onions, basil and 1/4 cup mint in a bowl and mix well. Add the coconut milk, soy sauce, turmeric, Chinese chili sauce and salt and mix well. Pour into the reserved drippings in the roasting pan. Bring to a low boil over high heat, stirring to deglaze the pan. Reduce the heat. Add enough of the cornstarch mixture gradually to lightly thicken the sauce, stirring constantly. Adjust the seasonings. Return the chicken to the roasting pan and coat with the sauce. Arrange on heated serving plates. Garnish with sprigs of fresh mint.

Yield: 8 servings

Chicken Cutlets with Lime

4 boneless chicken breasts
3/4 cup dry bread crumbs
1 tablespoon minced tarragon
1/2 teaspoon salt
1/4 teaspoon pepper
1 egg, beaten
2 tablespoons olive oil
2 tablespoons unsalted butter
1 lime, cut into wedges

Pound each chicken breast into a 6×8-inch piece. Mix the bread crumbs, tarragon, salt and pepper in a bowl. Dip the chicken into the egg. Dredge in the bread crumb mixture to coat. Arrange on a wire rack. Chill, covered, in the refrigerator for 1 hour. Sauté the chicken in the olive oil and butter in a skillet for 1 to 2 minutes on each side or until cooked through. Do not overcook. Garnish with lime wedges.

Yield: 4 servings

Quick and Easy Chicken Dubonnet

8 boneless skinless chicken breasts
1/3 cup all-purpose flour
1 tablespoon salt
1/4 cup (1/2 stick) butter
3/4 cup white Dubonnet
3 tablespoons soy sauce
1 teaspoon confectioners' sugar

Coat the chicken with the flour and salt. Brown in the butter in a skillet. Arrange in a single layer in a baking pan. Heat the Dubonnet, soy sauce and confectioners' sugar in a saucepan until the confectioners' sugar dissolves, stirring occasionally. Pour over the chicken. Bake at 350 degrees for 50 minutes or until the chicken is cooked through.

Yield: 6 to 8 servings

Magnificent Marinated Chicken

1/2 cup peanut oil
1/2 cup lemon juice
1/2 cup soy sauce
1 teaspoon salt
1 teaspoon garlic powder
2 tablespoons
  Worcestershire sauce

8 dashes of Tabasco sauce,
  or to taste
3 tablespoons chopped
  green onions
6 to 12 chicken breasts, or
  20 to 30 chicken strips

Process the peanut oil, lemon juice, soy sauce, salt, garlic powder, Worcestershire sauce, Tabasco sauce and green onions in a blender until blended. Pour over the chicken in a sealable plastic food storage bag and seal the bag. Marinate in the refrigerator for 12 to 30 hours. Drain the chicken, discarding the marinade. Arrange on a grill rack. Grill over hot coals until the chicken is cooked through.

Yield: 6 to 12 servings

Florida Gulf Coast BBQ Shrimp

3 pounds large Gulf
  shrimp
1 cup (2 sticks) butter
1/4 cup Worcestershire
  sauce
1 tablespoon olive oil
1 tablespoon lemon juice
2 garlic cloves, minced

2 bay leaves
1 tablespoon thyme
2 teaspoons Crazy Jane's
  seasoned salt or Tony
  Chachere's Seasoning
1 teaspoon salt
1 teaspoon pepper

Rinse the shrimp and arrange in a large broiler pan. Combine the butter, Worcestershire sauce, olive oil, lemon juice, garlic, bay leaves, thyme, seasoned salt, salt and pepper in a saucepan. Cook over medium heat until the butter melts, stirring frequently. Pour over the shrimp. Bake at 400 degrees for 12 to 17 minutes or until shrimp begin to change color. Broil for 3 minutes longer or until the shrimp turns pink; do not overcook. Cool in the pan. Peel and serve with Cheese Grits (page 87), homegrown tomatoes and garlic bread.

Yield: 6 to 8 servings

Paul Prudhomme tells us to cook shrimp with the heads on if possible. The fat (the orange substance in the heads) adds flavor and makes shrimp dishes rich, full, and sweet tasting.

Shrimp and Grits

1 pound large shrimp, peeled, deveined
1/2 cup Wondra flour
1 tablespoon peanut oil
6 slices bacon, chopped
1/2 cup sliced mushrooms
2 garlic cloves, peeled
2 teaspoons fresh lemon juice
1/4 teaspoon Tabasco sauce, or to taste
2/3 cup chopped scallions
Salt and pepper to taste
Cheese Grits (below)

Dredge the shrimp in the flour. Heat the peanut oil in a skillet or sauté pan. Add the bacon. Cook over low heat until the bacon is nearly crisp. Remove the bacon with a slotted spoon to a plate lined with paper towels to drain. Increase the heat to medium. Arrange the shrimp in a single layer in the skillet. Cook for 2 minutes. Add the mushrooms and turn the shrimp. Cook for 2 minutes. Squeeze the garlic into the mixture using a garlic press and stir. Stir in the lemon juice and Tabasco sauce. Add the scallions and cooked bacon. Season with salt and pepper. Serve hot over hot Cheese Grits.

Yield: 4 servings

Cheese Grits

4 1/2 cups water
1 teaspoon salt
1 cup quick-cooking grits
1 tablespoon butter
1/2 to 3/4 cup shredded Cheddar cheese
1/4 cup grated Parmesan cheese

Bring the water and salt to a boil in a heavy 3-quart saucepan. Add the grits gradually, whisking constantly. Reduce the heat to low. Continue to cook until only an occasional bubble breaks the surface, whisking constantly. Continue to cook for 7 to 11 minutes, stirring frequently. Stir in the butter, Cheddar cheese and Parmesan cheese. Serve immediately.

Save some clam shells from your next beach outing. They're great for serving small amounts of melted butter or other dipping sauces. Children especially love to be served from a shell.

A small amount of good olive oil, added after heating, greatly improves the flavor of canned tomato soup.

Classic Bouillabaisse

1/4 cup olive oil
1 rib celery
1 medium onion, chopped
1 leek, chopped
1 garlic clove, pressed
1/2 teaspoon thyme
1/2 bay leaf
2 cups crushed tomatoes
1 (8-ounce) bottle clam juice
1 cup dry white wine
1/2 teaspoon crushed fennel seeds
Few threads of saffron
2 tablespoons chopped parsley
Salt and pepper to taste
Meat of 1 small lobster, cut up
12 mussels
12 shrimp, peeled, deveined
12 scallops
1 pound orange roughy or other firm white fish

Heat the olive oil in a large stockpot. Add the celery, onion, leek, garlic, thyme and bay leaf. Cook for 5 minutes. Add the tomatoes, clam juice, wine, fennel seeds, saffron, parsley, salt and pepper. Cook for 15 minutes. Add the seafood. Cook for 15 minutes or until the lobster is opaque, the mussel shells open, the shrimp turn pink and the scallops are tender. Discard the bay leaf before serving. Serve with small rounds of French bread sautéed lightly in olive oil with garlic.

Yield: 4 servings

Crunchy Catfish

2 large eggs, beaten
2 tablespoons water
$1/2$ cup crushed saltine crackers
$1/4$ cup grated Parmesan cheese
1 tablespoon Cavender's Greek seasoning
1 teaspoon thyme
1 teaspoon basil
4 large catfish fillets
2 tablespoons unsalted butter, melted

Beat the eggs and water in a bowl. Combine the crackers, Parmesan cheese, Greek seasoning, thyme and basil in a shallow dish and mix well. Dip the fish in the egg mixture. Dredge in the crumb mixture. Arrange in a greased baking pan. Drizzle with the butter. Bake at 325 degrees for 30 minutes or until the fish flakes easily.

Note: You may assemble early in the day, refrigerate and bake later. You may also use tilapia fillets instead of catfish.

Yield: 4 servings

One of the joys of living in a small town is reading the small town newspaper. Some folks write "Local" columns. The following is an excerpt: "The summer has come and gone. The vegetables have gone. What leaves that are on the trees are all brown. The frost has killed the flowers. Next will be snow and ice. It's real cold when the wind blows. It's winter in the mountains."

Salmon with Arugula, Tomato and Caper Sauce

1 pound plum tomatoes, seeded, chopped
3/4 cup lightly packed chopped fresh arugula
1 shallot, chopped
1/2 cup olive oil
1 1/2 tablespoons lemon juice
1 tablespoon drained capers
4 (6-ounce) salmon fillets
1/4 cup olive oil
Salt and pepper to taste

Combine the tomatoes, arugula, shallot, 1/2 cup olive oil, lemon juice and capers in a bowl and mix well. Brush both sides of the fish with 1/4 cup olive oil. Season with salt and pepper. Arrange on a rack in a broiler pan. Broil for 4 minutes or just until the fish flakes easily; do not turn. Arrange on serving plates. Spoon the tomato mixture over the fish. Garnish with lemon wedges.

Yield: 4 servings

Arugula is very easy to grow. You can pick it very soon after planting and add it to a salad. This is also true of mustard, which you can grow indoors by sprinkling seeds on damp paper towels. Mustard, with its cress-like tiny green leaves, makes a lovely garnish on just about anything.

Salmon with Creamy Lime Sauce

4 (5-ounce) salmon fillets
1 tablespoon tequila
1 tablespoon lime juice
$^1/_2$ cup sour cream
2 tablespoons chopped fresh parsley
1 tablespoon chopped chives
$^1/_2$ teaspoon lime zest
Dash of salt
Dash of white pepper
2 tablespoons whipped butter, melted

Arrange the fish in a single layer in a large glass or stainless steel container. Mix the tequila and lime juice in a small bowl. Pour over the fish, turning to coat. Cover with plastic wrap. Marinate in the refrigerator for 30 minutes. Process the sour cream, parsley, chives, lime zest, salt and pepper in a blender until smooth.

Drain the fish, reserving the marinade. Arrange the fish on a rack in a broiler pan. Combine the reserved marinade and butter in a bowl and mix well. Broil the fish for 3 to 4 minutes or until the fish flakes easily, basting with the marinade mixture. Remove the fish to a serving platter. Pour any juices from the broiler pan and any remaining marinade mixture over the fish. Spoon the lime sauce over the top. Garnish with lemon and lime slices and sprigs of fresh flat-leaf parsley.

Yield: 4 servings

Dill adds a special zest to salmon. Its seeds perk up canned green beans.

Broil fish on top of shredded lettuce or celery or carrots. This makes cleanup easier and imparts flavor as well.

Dr. Robert Zahner
in his book
Mountain at the End
of the Trail *explains
the bear shadow
that can be seen
from the Big View
at Cowee Gap:
"Twice each year
the spirit of the
great black bear
of Whiteside
Mountain comes
to the Chattooga
River Valley below
the mountain. For
two weeks in mid-
October and again
in late February,
just before sunset
each afternoon the
famous shadow of
the bear stretches
across the valley
from the Devil's
Courthouse to
Timber Ridge."*

Grilled Swordfish with Avocado Butter

3 pounds thickly sliced swordfish fillets
Lemon juice to taste
Melted butter to taste
Soy sauce to taste
Avocado Butter (below)

Brush the fish with lemon juice, butter and soy sauce. Arrange
on a grill rack. Grill over hot coals until the fish flakes easily,
basting frequently with lemon juice, butter and soy sauce.
Serve with Avocado Butter.

Yield: 6 servings

Avocado Butter

1/2 cup (1 stick) butter, softened
1/4 cup mashed avocado (seed reserved)
1 tablespoon lemon juice
1 teaspoon Worcestershire sauce
1/2 teaspoon garlic salt
1/2 teaspoon barbecue spice

Whip the butter in a small bowl until smooth and creamy.
Fold in the avocado, lemon juice, Worcestershire sauce, garlic
salt and barbecue spice. Place the reserved avocado seed in
the center to prevent turning brown. Chill, covered, until
ready to use. Remove the avocado seed before serving.

Yield: 3/4 cup

Mountain Trout (Three Ways)

1/4 cup olive oil
1/4 cup fresh tarragon or any favorite herb
1/4 cup lemon juice
1/2 teaspoon salt
2 (2-pound) dressed trout
4 sprigs of fresh tarragon or any favorite herb
1 lemon, sliced

Cook the olive oil and tarragon in a small saucepan over low heat for 20 minutes. Pour through a wire-mesh strainer, discarding the solids. Combine the olive oil mixture, lemon juice and salt in a bowl and whisk well. Brush 1/2 of the mixture inside each fish. Stuff 2 sprigs of tarragon and 2 lemon slices inside each fish. Arrange the fish in a large dish. Pour the remaining olive oil mixture over the fish. Marinate, covered, in the refrigerator for 2 hours. Drain the fish and place in a grill basket coated with nonstick cooking spray. Grill, covered with the grill lid, over hot coals for 5 minutes on each side or until the fish flakes easily.

Yield: 4 servings

For Baked Trout, prepare the fish as directed above. Bake at 350 degrees for 30 minutes or until the fish flakes easily. Do not turn the fish during baking.

For Poached Trout, stuff the tarragon sprigs and lemon slices inside each fish. Wrap each fish in 3 layers of cheesecloth. Combine 4 cups water and 2 cups dry white wine in a fish poacher or oblong Dutch oven. Bring to a boil over high heat and reduce the heat. Add the fish. Simmer, covered, for 20 minutes or until the fish flakes easily. Remove and discard the cheesecloth. Prepare the olive oil and lemon juice mixture as directed for Mountain Trout (Three Ways) and serve with the fish.

The Highlands Biological Station is one of Highlands' greatest treasures. It came into existence in 1927. Two reasons for its location in the Highlands area are Highlands' unique bio-diversity and temperate climate. Ran Shaffner in his history of Highlands says: "... the Highlands Biological Station has opened in this small mountain town a unique window on the natural world, allowing local citizens and visiting scientists to appreciate and enjoy more fully and profoundly the loveliest of rare environments."

Tuna à la Dana

2 pounds fresh tuna steaks
1 large gingerroot, peeled, grated
4 garlic cloves, minced
Juice of 2 fresh medium limes
2 tablespoons soy sauce
2 tablespoons vegetable oil

Arrange the fish in a baking dish. Mix the gingerroot, garlic, lime juice, soy sauce and oil in a small bowl. Pour over the fish. Cover with foil. Marinate in the refrigerator for 1 hour. Bake, covered with foil, at 350 degrees for 14 minutes. Uncover and increase the oven temperature to 400 degrees. Bake for 3 to 5 minutes longer or until the fish flakes easily. Serve with the pan drippings.

Yield: 4 servings

Fish in a Dish

3 tablespoons butter
1 pound white fish, such as sea bass or halibut
1 large lemon, cut into halves
1/2 cup white wine Worcestershire sauce
Lemon pepper and paprika to taste

Melt the butter in a glass baking dish in a 350-degree oven. Arrange the fish in the butter, turning to coat both sides. Squeeze 1 lemon half over the fish and douse with 1/2 of the Worcestershire sauce. Sprinkle with lemon pepper and paprika. Turn the fish. Repeat the process with the remaining lemon half, Worcestershire sauce, lemon pepper and paprika. Bake at 350 degrees for 10 minutes per inch of thickness or until the fish flakes easily. Do not turn. Serve with hot cooked rice and lemon wedges.

Yield: 2 servings

94

Tabasco Mayonnaise

2 cups mayonnaise
2 tablespoons olive oil
1 tablespoon lemon juice
18 dashes of Tabasco sauce
Pinch of black pepper
1 teaspoon celery salt
1/2 red bell pepper, roasted, chopped
1/4 cup olive oil

Combine the mayonnaise, 2 tablespoons olive oil, lemon juice, Tabasco sauce, pepper, celery salt and bell pepper in a blender or food processor. Add 1/4 cup olive oil in a fine stream, processing constantly. Pour into a container. Chill, covered, until ready to serve. Serve over fillets, crab cakes or fried green tomatoes.

Yield: 2¹/₂ cups

Cajun Spice Rub for Fish

2 tablespoons coarsely ground black pepper
2 tablespoons dried lemon zest
1 tablespoon paprika
1 teaspoon tarragon
1 teaspoon basil
1/2 teaspoon cayenne pepper
1/4 teaspoon salt or salt substitute

Combine the black pepper, lemon zest, paprika, tarragon, basil, cayenne pepper and salt in a bowl and mix well. Store in an airtight container.

Yield: 6 tablespoons

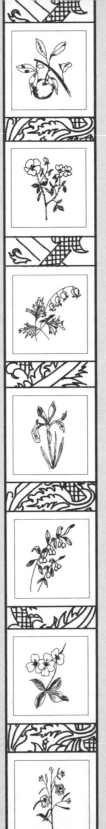

Ginger Lime Marinade for Swordfish

3 tablespoons canola oil
2 green onions, thinly sliced
1/4 cup fresh lime juice
1 tablespoon grated fresh gingerroot
Salt and pepper to taste

Heat the canola oil and green onions in a small saucepan over medium heat for 2 minutes. Stir in the lime juice, gingerroot, salt and pepper. Cook for 1 minute. Use to marinate swordfish in the refrigerator for at least 2 hours, turning halfway through. Let stand at room temperature for 30 minutes before grilling.

Yield: 3/4 cup

Ginger Soy Marinade

1/4 cup chopped green onions
1/4 cup toasted sesame oil
1/4 cup soy sauce or tamari
1/4 cup madeira or marsala
2 tablespoons honey
2 tablespoons minced garlic
1 tablespoon minced fresh gingerroot

Combine the green onions, sesame oil, soy sauce, wine, honey, garlic and gingerroot in a bowl and mix well. Use to marinate beef or chicken in the refrigerator for 8 to 12 hours.

Yield: 1 1/4 cups

Squeeze bottles are also good to keep barbecue sauce in to squirt directly on the meat in the last part of cooking time. No yucky basting brush to wash.

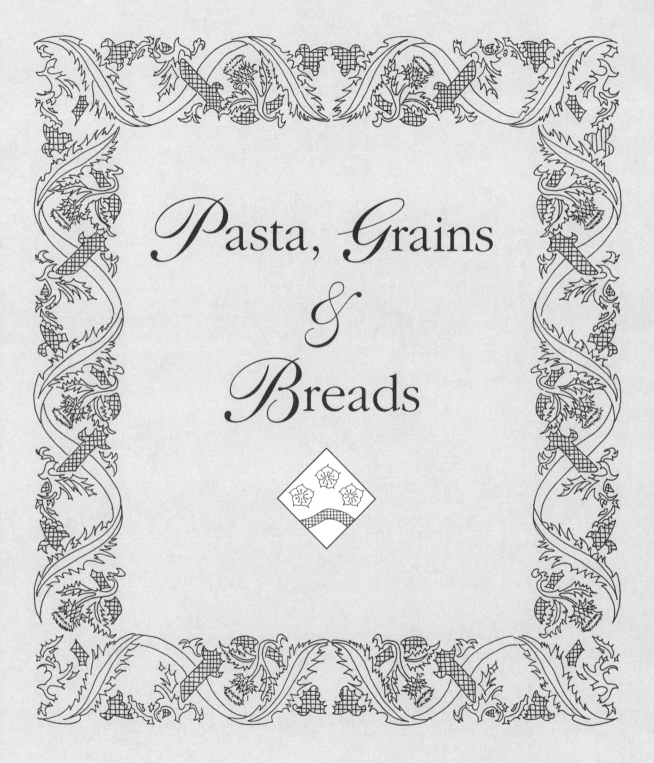

Pasta, Grains & Breads

Pasta with Sugar Snap Peas, Asparagus and Parmesan

1 pound asparagus, trimmed
Salt to taste
8 ounces bow-tie pasta
8 ounces sugar snap peas, trimmed
3 tablespoons olive oil
1/2 cup freshly grated Parmesan cheese
Pepper to taste

Cut the asparagus into 1 1/2-inch pieces. Add to boiling salted water in a large saucepan. Cook until tender-crisp. Remove immediately with a slotted spoon to cold water in a bowl. Cool slightly and drain. Add the pasta to the boiling water. Cook until al dente. Add the sugar snap peas. Boil for 2 minutes. Add the asparagus. Cook until heated through; drain. Add the olive oil and toss to coat. Add 1/2 cup Parmesan cheese. Season with salt and pepper. Serve with additional Parmesan cheese.

Yield: 4 servings

"Please pass the cheese." When garnishing pasta with a hard cheese like Parmigiano-Reggiano, do like the Italians do: Place a hunk of cheese on a beautiful pottery plate with a rasp grater and invite diners to grate their own.

Penne with Vodka and Spicy Tomato Sauce

2 Italian sausages (optional)
1/4 cup olive oil
4 garlic cloves, minced
1/2 teaspoon crushed red pepper flakes
1 (28-ounce) can crushed tomatoes
3/4 teaspoon fine sea salt
1 pound penne
2 tablespoons vodka
1/2 cup heavy cream
1/4 cup chopped fresh flat-leaf parsley

Remove the casings from the sausages. Brown the sausages in the hot olive oil in a large skillet, stirring until crumbly. Add the garlic and red pepper flakes. Cook until the garlic is brown, stirring constantly. Add the tomatoes and sea salt. Bring to a boil and reduce the heat. Simmer for 15 minutes.

Cook the pasta in a saucepan using the package directions. Drain well and return to the hot saucepan. Add the vodka and cream to the sauce. Bring to a boil. Add the sauce to the hot pasta and toss to mix. Cook over low heat for 1 minute. Stir in the parsley. Serve immediately.

Yield: 8 servings

Remember this when choosing which pasta goes with the sauce: The thicker the sauce, the larger the pasta.

Garlic Orange Couscous

1½ cups couscous
½ cup raisins
1 teaspoon turmeric
2 cups boiling water
1 (15-ounce) can chick-
   peas, rinsed, drained
2 medium tomatoes,
   chopped
⅔ cup sliced almonds,
   toasted

3 green onions, chopped
⅓ cup lemon juice
⅓ cup olive oil
2 garlic cloves, minced
Zest of 1 orange
1 tablespoon chopped
   fresh basil
½ teaspoon salt
Pepper to taste

Combine the couscous, raisins and turmeric in a heatproof bowl. Add the boiling water and mix well. Cover and let stand for 5 minutes. Uncover and fluff with a fork. Cover and let stand for 10 minutes. Stir in the chick-peas, tomatoes, almonds and green onions. Whisk the lemon juice, olive oil, garlic, orange zest, basil, salt and pepper in a large bowl. Add the couscous mixture and toss to mix. Chill, covered, for 1 to 12 hours. Serve on a bed of lettuce leaves.

Yield: 8 servings

Green and Yellow Rice

3 cups cooked rice
¼ cup (½ stick) butter,
   melted
4 eggs, beaten
1 cup milk
1 (10-ounce) package
   frozen chopped spinach,
   cooked, drained
1 pound sharp Cheddar
   cheese, shredded

1 tablespoon chopped
   onion
1 tablespoon
   Worcestershire sauce
½ teaspoon marjoram
½ teaspoon thyme
½ teaspoon rosemary
½ teaspoon salt

Mix the cooked rice and butter in a bowl. Beat the eggs and milk in a large bowl. Add the spinach and cheese and mix well. Stir in the onion, Worcestershire sauce, marjoram, thyme, rosemary and salt. Add the rice mixture and toss to mix. Spoon into a 2-quart baking dish sprayed with nonstick cooking spray. Set in a larger pan of warm water. Bake, uncovered, at 350 degrees for 45 minutes.

Yield: 8 servings

High Altitude Cooking: Water boiled in Highlands is not as hot as water boiled in Savannah. Therefore it is necessary to increase the cooking time. For instance, cook rice for 25 to 30 minutes rather than 20 to 25 minutes.

100

Rice and Green Chile Casserole

1 medium onion, chopped
1/2 cup (1 stick) butter
4 cups cooked rice
2 (4-ounce) cans chopped
   green chiles, drained
2 cups sour cream

1 cup cottage cheese
1 teaspoon salt
1/4 teaspoon pepper
8 ounces sharp Cheddar
   cheese, shredded

Sauté the onion in the butter in a skillet until transparent. Add the cooked rice, green chiles, sour cream, cottage cheese, salt and pepper and mix well. Spoon into a 2 1/2-quart baking dish. Sprinkle with the Cheddar cheese. Bake at 325 degrees for 20 minutes or until hot and bubbly.

Yield: 6 to 8 servings

Wild Rice Pilaf

1 cup wild rice
1 3/4 cups chicken or
   vegetable stock
1/3 cup dry vermouth
1 1/2 cups sliced fresh
   mushrooms
3/4 cup sliced celery
3/4 cup julienned carrots
3 tablespoons butter or
   margarine
1/3 cup sliced green
   onions

1 (10-ounce) package
   frozen artichoke hearts,
   thawed
2 tablespoons chopped red
   bell pepper
1 teaspoon lemon zest
1 tablespoon lemon juice
1/2 teaspoon thyme
1/4 teaspoon salt
1/4 teaspoon pepper

Rinse the rice in a colander under running water for 1 minute; drain. Combine the rice, stock and vermouth in a saucepan. Cook for 30 minutes. Remove from the heat. Do not drain.

Sauté the mushrooms, celery and carrots in 2 tablespoons of the butter in a skillet for 5 minutes. Add the remaining 1 tablespoon butter and remove from the heat. Stir in the rice mixture. Add the green onions, artichoke hearts, bell pepper, lemon zest, lemon juice, thyme, salt and pepper and mix well. Spoon into a greased 2-quart baking dish. Chill, covered, for up to 24 hours if desired. Bake, covered, at 325 degrees for 45 minutes, stirring once. Garnish with fresh chopped parsley.

Yield: 4 servings

The taste buds, which identify and appreciate different flavors, are in different parts of the mouth. A well-flavored dish has a "roundness in the mouth." For instance, black pepper, white pepper, and red pepper may all be used in a dish that requires pepper. The three will light up different parts of your mouth, creating that "round" taste of a really superb dish.

More about pepper: black is for flavor, white is for bite, and red is for heat.

Rosemary Buttermilk Bread

3³/4 teaspoons dry yeast
1 cup warm water
6³/4 cups all-purpose flour
1 tablespoon salt
1 cup buttermilk

¹/3 cup olive oil
¹/4 cup finely chopped
 rosemary
Coarse salt

Dissolve the yeast in warm water in a bowl. Let stand for
10 minutes. Combine the flour and salt in a food processor.
Add the buttermilk, olive oil, rosemary and yeast. Process
to form a smooth and nonsticky dough. Place in a greased
bowl, turning to coat the surface. Cover with plastic wrap.
Let rise for 1¹/2 hours. Divide the dough into 2 equal portions.
Shape each portion into a loaf. Place in greased 5×8-inch
loaf pans. Let rise for 1 hour. Cut the surface of the dough
diagonally and sprinkle with coarse salt. Bake at 425 degrees
for 20 to 30 minutes or until the loaves test done.

Yield: 2 loaves

*Grow the annual
Nigella, "Love-
in-a-Mist," for its
beautiful lacy
flowers and
decorative seedpods.
Harvest some of
those seeds for
future planting,
and use the rest to
sprinkle on bread-
sticks or rolls. The
seeds, for some
reason, are called
black onion seeds.*

Cranberries and Cream Bread

1¹/2 cups (3 sticks) butter,
 softened
3 cups sugar
6 eggs
2 cups sour cream
1 tablespoon vanilla
 extract

2 tablespoons orange zest
6 cups all-purpose flour
1¹/2 teaspoons baking
 powder
1 teaspoon baking soda
1¹/2 teaspoons salt
4 cups whole cranberries

Cream the butter and sugar in a mixing bowl until light and
fluffy. Add the eggs, sour cream, vanilla and orange zest and
mix well. Beat in the flour, baking powder, baking soda and
salt until smooth. Fold in the cranberries. Pour into 4 greased
and floured 4×8-inch loaf pans, smoothing over the tops.
Bake at 350 degrees for 1 hour or until the loaves test done.

Yield: 4 loaves

*Note: You may use 2 teaspoons orange or lemon extract
instead of the orange zest. This bread also freezes well.*

Sour Cream Corn Bread

2 eggs
1 cup canned cream-style corn
1 cup sour cream
$1/2$ cup corn oil or canola oil
1 cup cornmeal
1 tablespoon baking powder
$1^1/2$ teaspoons salt

Beat the eggs in a bowl with a whisk. Add the corn, sour cream and corn oil and mix well. Add the cornmeal, baking powder and salt and mix lightly. Pour into a greased number seven cast-iron skillet. Bake at 375 degrees for 20 minutes or until golden brown.

Yield: 8 servings

Note: You may add one 4-ounce can of chopped green chiles or jalapeños for more flavor.

Sage Cream Biscuits

2 cups self-rising flour
1 cup plus 1 tablespoon heavy cream
1 tablespoon chopped sage

Combine the flour, cream and sage in a bowl and stir with a fork just until the flour is moistened. Turn onto a lightly floured surface. Knead lightly 5 or 6 times or just until the dough holds together. Roll gently into a circle 1 to 2 inches thick. Cut with a 2-inch biscuit cutter. Arrange on an ungreased baking sheet. Bake at 425 degrees for 10 to 12 minutes or until golden brown.

Yield: 14 to 16 biscuits

Ham biscuits. Order center slices of old Kentucky ham directly from Critchfield's in Nicholasville, Kentucky, by calling 1-800-86-MEATS. Buy frozen biscuits (the big ones) from Dusty Rhodes' Superette.

If your recipe calls for self-rising flour and all you have is all-purpose flour, remove 1 teaspoon from a cup of flour and add 1 teaspoon baking powder and 1/2 teaspoon salt. You will have a cup of self-rising flour. However, don't try to substitute self-rising flour for all-purpose flour. The result will be all over your oven.

Sweet Potato Biscuits

2 cups mashed cooked sweet potatoes
1/2 cup (1 stick) butter, melted
1 1/4 cups milk
4 cups self-rising flour
Pinch of baking powder
3 tablespoons sugar

Combine the sweet potatoes, butter and milk in a bowl and mix well. Stir in the flour, baking powder and sugar. Turn onto a lightly floured surface. Knead 8 to 10 times or until the dough holds together. Roll into a circle 1 inch thick. Cut with a biscuit cutter. Arrange on a greased baking sheet. Bake at 400 degrees for 15 to 20 minutes or until brown.

Yield: 2 dozen biscuits

Christmas Morning Rolls

1 (24-count) package frozen yeast rolls
1 (4-ounce) package butterscotch cook-and-serve
    pudding mix
1/2 cup chopped pecans
1/2 cup (1 stick) butter
3/4 cup packed brown sugar
3/4 teaspoon cinnamon

Arrange the frozen rolls in a greased tube pan. Sprinkle with the pudding mix and pecans. Cook the butter, brown sugar and cinnamon in a saucepan over low heat until the brown sugar melts and the mixture barely bubbles, stirring frequently. Pour over the rolls in the prepared pan. Cover tightly with foil. Let stand at room temperature for 8 to 12 hours. Bake, uncovered, at 350 degrees for 24 to 30 minutes or until golden brown. Invert onto a serving plate.

Yield: 24 servings

Roast Beef in Pita Pockets

2 pounds cooked roast beef, thinly sliced
1 cup sour cream
1 teaspoon dillweed
1/4 cup chopped green onions
1/4 cup olive oil
1/4 cup dry red wine
1 tablespoon vinegar
1 teaspoon basil
1/2 teaspoon salt
1 pound sliced fresh mushrooms
2 large tomatoes, coarsely chopped
1/2 cup sliced green onions
8 pita pockets, split

Chill the roast beef. Combine the sour cream, dillweed and
1/4 cup green onions in a bowl and mix well. Chill, covered,
for 3 to 12 hours.

Blend the olive oil, red wine, vinegar, basil and salt in a bowl.
Combine the mushrooms, tomatoes and 1/2 cup green onions
in a bowl. Add the olive oil mixture and toss to coat. Chill,
covered, for 3 to 12 hours.

To assemble, spread the inside of the pita pockets with some
of the sour cream mixture. Place several slices of roast beef
in the pita pockets. Top with the vegetable mixture. Add any
remaining sour cream mixture if desired.

Yield: 8 servings

*Check the
wildflower trails
around the
Botanical Gardens
regularly. There's
always a surprise.
Children love the
wooden bridges
and the lily pond
where frogs
jump in at their
approach. Catch
a bug and feed
it to one of the
carnivorous pitcher
plants that grow in
the bog. Cranberries
grow there too.*

Vidalia Onion Sandwiches

Firm white bread, thinly sliced
Mayonnaise
Vidalia onions, thinly sliced
Salt and freshly ground pepper to taste
Minced fresh parsley

Cut the bread into circles, discarding the crust. Coat one side of each circle with mayonnaise. Arrange 1 onion slice on the top of 1/2 of the bread circles. Sprinkle with salt and pepper. Top with the remaining bread circles mayonnaise side down. Brush the edge of each sandwich with mayonnaise. Roll each edge in parsley. Arrange on a serving platter. Cover with a damp towel until ready to serve.

Yield: variable

U-Pick Tomato Sandwiches

4 loaves dry sandwich bread
6 to 8 medium tomatoes
Salt and pepper to taste
Mayonnaise
1 onion, grated
Paprika to taste

Cut the bread with a biscuit cutter into 72 circles, reserving the trimmings for another purpose. Drop the tomatoes into boiling water in a saucepan. Boil for exactly 28 seconds; drain. Peel the tomatoes. Cut into thin slices and arrange on paper towels to drain. Season with salt and pepper.

Spread mayonnaise on one side of each bread round. Arrange the drained tomato slices on 1/2 of the bread rounds. Sprinkle with salt and pepper. Sprinkle 1/2 teaspoon undrained grated onion over each tomato. Top with the remaining bread rounds mayonnaise side down. Sprinkle with paprika. Arrange on a tray, placing waxed paper between each layer. Store, tightly covered, in the refrigerator until ready to serve.

Yield: 36 servings

Eggs, Cheese & Brunch

Early Inns of
Highlands:

• The Highlands
House, now
Highlands Inn, is
on the National
Register, as is the
Central House or
Old Edwards Inn.

• Islington House
later became King's
Inn, but that lovely
old hotel burned in
the early 1990s.
During its heyday,
the food served by
Mrs. King was
unforgettable.

• Davis House was
perhaps the most
elegant inn. It
changed owners
and names many
times. The Davis
House became The
Martin, Tricemont
Terrace, Bascom
House and King's
Inn II, and finally
Lee's Inn. Lee's Inn
burned in 1972
and The Kelsey and
Hutchinson Lodge
has been built on
the old site.

Baked Eggs with Onions and Cheese

1/4 cup (1/2 stick) butter
4 cups sliced onions
1 cup plain bread crumbs
2 cups grated Cheddar cheese
8 eggs
Salt and freshly ground pepper to taste

Heat the butter in a large skillet over medium heat for
2 minutes. Add the onions. Cook for 15 minutes or until the
onions are soft but not brown, stirring occasionally. Spread
over the bottom of a 9×13-inch baking dish. Layer 1/2 of the
bread crumbs and 1/2 of the cheese over the onions. Make
8 little nests with the back of a spoon in the layers. Crack
1 egg into each nest. Sprinkle with salt and pepper. Layer the
remaining bread crumbs and remaining cheese over the top.
Bake at 350 degrees for 15 to 20 minutes or until the eggs
are set. Serve with toast.

Yield: 4 to 8 servings

Southwestern Eggs

10 eggs
1/2 cup (1 stick) butter, melted
1/2 cup all-purpose flour
1 teaspoon baking powder
2 cups cottage cheese
2 (4-ounce) cans chopped green chiles, drained
1 teaspoon salt
1 pound Monterey Jack cheese, shredded

Whisk the eggs in a large bowl. Add the butter, flour, baking
powder, cottage cheese, green chiles and salt and whisk well.
Fold in the cheese. Pour into a 9×13-inch baking dish sprayed
with nonstick cooking spray. Bake at 350 degrees for 40 to
45 minutes or until set.

Yield: 8 to 10 servings

Cheesy Jalapeño Pie

1 (7-ounce) can jalapeños, drained
8 ounces sharp Cheddar cheese, shredded
4 eggs
Salt and pepper to taste

Remove the seeds from the chiles. Cut the chiles into thin slivers. Line the bottom and side of a 9-inch pie plate with the chiles. Press the cheese over the chiles. Beat the eggs, salt and pepper in a bowl until blended. Pour over the cheese layer. Bake at 350 degrees for 25 to 30 minutes or until set. Cut into wedges to serve.

Yield: 6 to 8 servings

Sweet Onion Tart

1 cup crushed butter crackers
1/4 cup (1/2 stick) butter, melted
3 cups chopped sweet onions
2 1/2 tablespoons butter
2 eggs
3/4 cup milk
1 teaspoon salt
1/2 teaspoon pepper
1 1/4 cups shredded cheese
1/8 teaspoon Hungarian paprika

Mix the cracker crumbs and 1/4 cup melted butter in a bowl. Press into a greased 9-inch pie plate. Sauté the onions in 2 1/2 tablespoons butter in a skillet until transparent. Spoon into the prepared pie plate. Beat the eggs, milk, salt and pepper in a bowl until blended. Pour over the onion layer. Sprinkle with the cheese and paprika. Bake at 350 degrees for 30 minutes or until set.

Yield: 6 to 8 servings

Early Inns of Highlands:

• The Hall House was built in 1888. In the late 1920s and early '30s, if you gazed from where Wild Thyme is on Fifth Street toward Sixth Street, you would see a lovely nine-hole golf course, a lake, and The Hall House appearing to float shiplike on green, manicured grounds with a backdrop of pines, hemlocks, and Sunset Rock.

Tomato Basil Tart

1 refrigerator pie pastry	4 garlic cloves
1/2 cup shredded mozzarella cheese	1 cup shredded mozzarella cheese
5 Roma or 4 medium tomatoes, sliced	1/2 cup mayonnaise
1 cup loosely packed fresh basil leaves	1/4 cup grated Parmesan cheese
	1/8 teaspoon white pepper

Line a 9-inch tart pan or pie plate with the pastry, trimming and fluting the edge. Bake using the package directions. Remove from the oven. Sprinkle immediately with 1/2 cup mozzarella cheese. Cool on a wire rack. Arrange the tomatoes on the melted cheese. Process the basil and garlic in a food processor until coarsely chopped. Spread over the tomatoes. Combine 1 cup mozzarella cheese, mayonnaise, Parmesan cheese and white pepper in a medium mixing bowl and mix well. Spoon over the basil mixture, spreading evenly to the edge to cover the top. Bake at 375 degrees for 25 to 40 minutes or until the top is golden brown and bubbly.

Note: Do not use fat-free mayonnaise in this recipe.

Yield: 6 to 8 servings

Artichoke Rarebit

1/2 cup (1 stick) butter	1 (8-ounce) can water chestnuts, drained
3 ounces dried chipped beef	1 (10-ounce) package frozen artichoke hearts, cooked, drained, cut into pieces
1/2 cup all-purpose flour	
2 cups cream	1/4 cup dry vermouth
3 cups milk	5 large croissants, split into halves, or buttered toast points
Salt and pepper to taste	
8 ounces sharp Cheddar cheese, shredded	

Melt the butter in a skillet. Add the beef. Sauté briefly. Add the flour and stir until sauce is smooth. Stir in the cream. Add the milk, salt, pepper, cheese, water chestnuts, artichoke hearts and vermouth in the order listed, stirring well after each addition. Cook until bubbly. Serve over croissant halves or buttered toast points.

Yield: 10 servings

BLT Morning Pizza

1 (10-count) can flaky biscuits
6 slices bacon, cooked
2 medium tomatoes, peeled, seeded, chopped, drained
1/2 small onion, chopped
3 ounces Swiss cheese, shredded
1/2 cup mayonnaise
2 teaspoons basil

Pull the biscuit dough apart. Arrange the dough in a 9×13-inch baking pan sprayed with nonstick cooking spray. Combine the bacon, tomatoes, onion, cheese, mayonnaise and basil in a bowl and mix well. Spread on top of the dough. Bake at 375 degrees for 25 to 30 minutes or until bubbly. Cut into squares to serve.

Yield: 8 servings

Giddy Up Grits

1 pound bulk pork sausage
1 garlic clove, minced
1 teaspoon hot sauce
3/4 teaspoon pepper
4 cups water
1 cup quick-cooking grits
2 eggs
2 cups shredded sharp Cheddar cheese
1 (7-ounce) can diced green chiles, drained
1/2 cup chopped red bell pepper
1/3 cup fresh cilantro leaves

Brown the sausage in a skillet, stirring until crumbly; drain. Add the garlic, hot sauce and pepper and mix well. Bring the water to a boil in a saucepan and reduce the heat. Add the grits gradually, stirring constantly. Cook for 5 to 6 minutes or until the grits are tender.

Beat the eggs in a large bowl. Add the Cheddar cheese, green chiles, sausage and grits and mix well. Pour into a 9×13-inch or 2 1/2- to 3-quart buttered baking dish. Bake, uncovered, at 350 degrees for 45 minutes. Let stand for 5 minutes. Sprinkle with the bell pepper and cilantro.

Yield: 8 to 10 servings

111

The Dugout on Lake Sequoyah was once "The Mint," where Civil War souvenirs and coins were sold. But prior to that it was a tavern where wine and beer could be bought. The Dugout was frequented by the "racy" sophisticated crowd, and it is said its customers drank, danced, partied, and gambled the night away.

Granola

1/4 cup vegetable oil
2/3 cup honey
3 cups old-fashioned rolled oats
1/4 tablespoon cinnamon
1/3 cup unsweetened flaked coconut
1/2 cup sliced almonds
1/2 cup macadamia nuts, coarsely chopped
1/2 cup sunflower kernels
1/2 cup raisins
1/4 cup dried cranberries
1/2 cup dried apricots, coarsely chopped

Heat the oil and honey in a small saucepan until blended.
Combine the oats, cinnamon, coconut, almonds, macadamia
nuts and sunflower kernels in a large bowl. Add the honey
mixture and stir to coat. Spread in a 10×15-inch baking pan.
Bake at 300 degrees for 10 minutes. Stir the mixture. Bake for
5 to 10 minutes longer, stirring after 5 minutes. Do not brown.
Remove from the oven and cool briefly. Stir in the raisins,
cranberries and apricots. Let stand until cooled completely.
Store in an airtight container. Use to sprinkle over fresh fruit
or in pancake batter.

Yield: 12 servings

There were families who brought their horses to Highlands with them in the summer. One method of transporting the horses was to load them on a train, perhaps in Birmingham, Atlanta, or New Orleans, bound for Clayton, Georgia, or Seneca, South Carolina, and then drive up and meet the train. It was easy to ride the horses from there on to Highlands to be enjoyed all summer.

Parmesan Pita Toasts

1 package pita bread
3 tablespoons butter, softened
1/4 cup grated Parmesan cheese

Split each pita round in half. Cut each round into halves. Cut the halves into 2 triangles. Spread each triangle lightly with butter. Sprinkle with Parmesan cheese. Place on a baking sheet. Broil for 2 to 3 minutes or until light brown.

Yield: 8 servings

Quick Pickled Peaches

1 (29-ounce) can yellow cling peach halves
3/4 cup packed brown sugar
1/2 cup vinegar
2 to 3 cinnamon sticks
1 teaspoon whole cloves
1 teaspoon allspice

Drain the peaches, reserving the liquid. Combine the reserved liquid, brown sugar, vinegar, cinnamon sticks, cloves and allspice in a saucepan. Bring to a boil. Boil for 5 minutes, stirring constantly. Add the peaches and reduce the heat. Simmer for 5 minutes. Remove from the heat. Let stand, covered, for 6 to 8 hours. Chill, covered, in the refrigerator until ready to serve.

Yield: 4 to 6 servings

Peach halves are delicious barbecued. Sprinkle peaches with ginger and brown sugar, thread on skewers, and grill until the sugar caramelizes. Serve with meat, fish, or poultry.

113

Amaze your friends: put a full-grown apple in a bottle. Use a small, squat juice bottle with about a one-inch opening. When your apple tree has just set fruit and apples are the size of a small marble, carefully position the bottle over the fruit and its branch. Carefully tape around the neck of the bottle and the branch so that the bottle hangs from the tree. Make it watertight. Do five or six of these, as the success rate is not high. Watch the apple grow inside the bottle. When the apple is full grown, fill the bottle with high proof vodka and cap. It's a real conversation piece on the bar.

Apple Butter

12 Granny Smith apples, peeled, chopped
2 cups sugar
1/4 cup apple cider vinegar
1/4 teaspoon cloves
1/2 teaspoon cinnamon
1/2 teaspoon allspice
Chopped nuts and raisins to taste

Combine the apples, sugar, vinegar, cloves, cinnamon, allspice, nuts and raisins in a slow cooker and mix well. Cook on Low for 24 hours.

Yield: 15 to 20 servings

Apricot Casserole

2 (16-ounce) cans apricots
15 butter crackers, crushed
1/2 cup packed brown sugar
3 tablespoons lemon juice
4 to 6 tablespoons butter
Cinnamon to taste

Drain the apricots, reserving the juice. Layer the apricots, crackers and brown sugar 1/3 at a time in a buttered 11/2-quart baking dish. Pour the reserved apricot juice and lemon juice over the top. Dot with butter. Sprinkle with cinnamon. Bake at 375 degrees for 40 minutes.

Yield: 8 servings

Desserts

Fabulous Flan

4 eggs
1 (14-ounce) can sweetened condensed milk
1 cup water
1 teaspoon vanilla extract
6 tablespoons dark brown sugar

Beat the eggs in a mixing bowl until light and fluffy. Add the condensed milk, water and vanilla and mix well. Spoon 1 tablespoon brown sugar into each of 6 custard cups. Pour the egg mixture carefully over the brown sugar. Arrange the custard cups in a pan of water. Bake at 350 degrees for 45 to 60 minutes or until a knife inserted in the custards comes out clean. Unmold onto serving plates. Garnish each with a fresh strawberry.

Yield: 6 servings

Perfect Poached Pears

6 Bosc pears or other firm pears
1 cup sugar
2 cups strong brewed coffee
1/2 cup whipping cream
2 tablespoons sugar

Peel the pears and trim the bottoms so each pear will stand up. Combine the pears, 1 cup sugar and coffee in a large saucepan. Poach over medium heat until the pears are tender. Remove the pears to a platter using a slotted spoon. Chill, covered, until ready to serve. Boil the remaining liquid until reduced and thickened. Remove from the heat. Do not chill the sauce. Beat the whipping cream and sugar in a mixing bowl until soft peaks form. To serve, arrange the pears on serving plates and drizzle with the sauce. Dollop with the whipped cream.

Yield: 6 servings

Lemon Ice Cream

1 cup sugar
Juice of 4 lemons
1 tablespoon grated lemon zest
Boiling water
3 eggs
1 cup sugar
2 cups milk, scalded
1 quart heavy cream

Combine 1 cup sugar, lemon juice and lemon zest in a heatproof bowl. Add enough boiling water to cover and stir until the sugar is dissolved. Mixe the eggs and 1 cup sugar in a double boiler. Add the milk gradually, stirring constantly. Cook over boiling water until smooth and thickened, stirring constantly. Remove from the heat to cool. Add the lemon mixture and cream and mix well. Pour into a 2-quart ice cream freezer container. Freeze using the manufacturer's instructions.

Yield: 2 quarts

Note: You may store the unfrozen mixture in the refrigerator for several days before freezing. Stir before freezing.

Peach Ice Cream

4 cups mashed peeled fresh peaches (about 8 large peaches)
1/2 cup sugar
4 cups milk
10 eggs, beaten
2 cups sugar
1/2 teaspoon salt
1 1/2 tablespoons cornstarch
4 cups half-and-half
2 teaspoons vanilla extract

Combine the peaches and 1/2 cup sugar in a bowl and toss to mix. Heat the milk in a saucepan until hot. Combine the eggs, 2 cups sugar, salt and cornstarch in a saucepan and mix well. Stir in 1/4 cup of the hot milk. Add the remaining hot milk and half-and-half and mix well. Cook over medium heat until the mixture coats a metal spoon, stirring constantly. Remove from the heat to cool. Stir in the peaches and vanilla. Chill for 2 to 12 hours. Pour into a 1-gallon ice cream freezer container. Freeze using the manufacturer's instructions. Let ripen for 1 to 1 1/2 hours before serving.

Yield: 1 gallon

Chamber Music Sundaes

3 oranges
1 cup packed light brown sugar
10 tablespoons fresh orange juice
3 tablespoons unsalted butter
Vanilla frozen yogurt or ice cream
1/2 cup hazelnuts, toasted, coarsely chopped

Remove the orange peel from the oranges. Cut enough of the peel into fine strips to measure 2 tablespoons. Combine the orange peel strips, brown sugar, orange juice and butter in a heavy medium saucepan. Cook over medium heat until the sugar dissolves, stirring constantly. Increase the heat to high. Boil gently for 15 minutes or until the mixture is reduced to 1 cup. Remove from the heat and cool to lukewarm.

Remove the pith from the oranges. Cut the oranges into rounds. Cut each round into quarters. Scoop the frozen yogurt into large wine glasses. Drizzle with the sauce. Top with the oranges and hazelnuts.

Yield: 6 servings

Ginger Mousse

4 cups whipping cream
1/2 cup sugar
2 teaspoons chopped green ginger
1 (8-ounce) can frozen shredded coconut
8 ounces chopped walnuts
9 tablespoons Drambuie
2 tablespoons Scotch
1 (16-ounce) package gingersnaps, broken up

Whip the cream in a mixing bowl. Add the sugar gradually, beating until soft peaks form. Add the ginger, coconut, walnuts, Drambuie and Scotch one at a time, whipping well after each addition. Alternate thick layers of the gingersnaps and whipped cream mixture in a large serving bowl until all ingredients are used, ending with the whipped cream mixture. Refrigerate until chilled through.

Yield: 10 servings

The ice cream cone was invented at the 1904 World's Fair by an enterprising ice cream vendor. When he ran out of cups, he sought the help of a nearby waffle vendor, and the rest is history.

Cold Lemon Soufflé

2 teaspoons unflavored gelatin
1/2 cup cold water
8 egg yolks
1 cup sugar
1 cup lemon juice
1 teaspoon salt
2 teaspoons lemon zest
8 egg whites
Pinch of cream of tartar
1 cup plus 2 tablespoons sugar

Tie a lightly greased collar of waxed paper around the outside of a 1¹/₂-quart soufflé dish so that the collar rises 3 inches above the top of the dish. Soften the gelatin in the cold water in a small bowl. Beat 8 egg yolks lightly in a double boiler. Add 1 cup sugar, lemon juice and salt. Cook over hot water until the mixture coats a spoon, stirring constantly. Add the lemon zest and the gelatin mixture and blend thoroughly. Remove from the heat to cool.

Beat the egg whites in a mixing bowl until soft peaks form. Add the cream of tartar and beat until stiff peaks form. Fold into the egg yolk mixture. Fold in 1 cup plus 2 tablespoons sugar. Pour into the prepared soufflé dish, filling 1¹/₂ inches below the top of the collar. Chill for 2 hours. Remove the collar just before serving. Serve with raspberry or strawberry sauce.

Yield: 8 servings

Learn to sauce the modern way: put the sauce on the plate, not the food. Use a squeeze bottle and draw the sauce on the plate from edge to edge in a decorative way.

Peach Rum Soufflé

1 tablespoon unflavored gelatin
1/4 cup cold water
1 cup peeled fresh peaches, puréed
1/2 cup confectioners' sugar
1 tablespoon dark rum
1 cup whipping cream
2 egg whites, stiffly beaten

Place an oiled waxed paper collar around an 8-inch soufflé dish. Soften the gelatin in cold water in a double boiler. Heat over hot water until dissolved, stirring constantly. Remove from the heat. Add the peaches, confectioners' sugar and rum. Whip the whipping cream in a bowl until soft peaks form. Fold into the stiffly beaten egg whites. Fold in the peach mixture. Spoon into the prepared soufflé dish. Chill for 4 hours or longer before serving.

Yield: 8 servings

Apple Torte

1/2 cup (1 stick) butter
1 cup all-purpose flour
2 tablespoons sugar
1/4 teaspoon salt
1 tablespoon white vinegar
5 or 6 unpeeled apples, cored, shredded
3/4 cup sugar
2 tablespoons all-purpose flour
1 teaspoon cinnamon

Cut the butter into 1 cup flour in a bowl until crumbly. Add 2 tablespoons sugar, salt and vinegar and mix well. Press over the bottom and 1 inch up the side of a 9-inch springform pan. Combine the apples, 3/4 cup sugar, 2 tablespoons flour and cinnamon in a bowl and toss to mix well. Pour into the prepared pan. Bake at 400 degrees for 45 minutes.

Yield: 12 servings

After a long, rich dinner, finish up with a dessert of cut up fruit (strawberries, peaches, melons, blueberries) served in a stemmed glass. Fill to the top with Asti Spumanti or your favorite sweet sparkling wine. Great sipping and spooning in the moonlight or beside the fire.

For a more stable pecan pie filling, add one tablespoon of flour to the custard mixture.

120

Raspberry Walnut Torte

1 cup all-purpose flour
1/3 cup confectioners' sugar
1/2 cup (1 stick) butter, softened
1 (10-ounce) package frozen raspberries, thawed
3/4 cup chopped walnuts
2 eggs
1 cup sugar
1/2 teaspoon salt
1/4 cup all-purpose flour
1/2 teaspoon baking powder
1 teaspoon vanilla extract
1/2 cup water
1/2 cup sugar
2 tablespoons cornstarch
1 tablespoon lemon juice
Whipped cream or ice cream

Combine 1 cup flour, confectioners' sugar and butter in a bowl and blend well. Press in a 9×13-inch baking pan. Bake at 350 degrees for 15 minutes. Remove from the oven to cool.

Drain the raspberries, reserving the liquid. Spoon the raspberries over the baked crust. Sprinkle with the walnuts. Beat the eggs and 1 cup sugar in a small mixing bowl until light and fluffy. Add the salt, 1/4 cup flour, baking powder and vanilla and beat well. Pour over the walnuts. Bake at 350 degrees for 30 to 35 minutes or until golden brown. Remove from the oven to cool.

Combine the water, reserved raspberry liquid, 1/2 cup sugar and cornstarch in a small saucepan. Cook until thickened and clear, stirring constantly. Stir in the lemon juice. Remove from the heat to cool.

To serve, cut the torte into squares. Serve with whipped cream and the raspberry sauce.

Yield: 12 servings

More High Altitude Cooking: Baked goods tend to rise faster, requiring a change in the proportion of ingredients used in breads, cakes, and muffins. Often the baking temperature needs to be increased by about 25 degrees. For yeast breads, watch the dough carefully and judge the rise time by the change in bulk.

For recipes using baking powder, decrease the amount of baking powder by about 1/8 teaspoon. Reduce sugar by about 1 tablespoon. Increase liquid by 1 to 2 tablespoons per cup. Don't overbeat the eggs. Raise the oven temperature slightly.

Grease pans well, as baked goods tend to stick more at high altitudes.

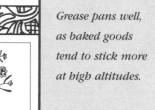

The Sullivan family's white picket fence encircled servant quarters, a windmill, tennis court, ice-house, and heather bed in the block that Carolina Way now intersects. The old house sat close to where Wild Thyme is today and faced Fifth Street. It was destroyed by developers in the '70s.

We are blessed to live in apple country. When making a pie, try using more than one variety of apples. It's lots more interesting.

Apple Harvest Cake

3 eggs
1 1/2 cups vegetable oil
2 cups sugar
3 cups all-purpose flour
1 teaspoon salt
1 teaspoon baking soda
2 teaspoons vanilla extract
1 teaspoon cinnamon
3 cups chopped unpeeled tart apples
1 1/3 cups chopped pecans
Topping (below)

Beat the eggs, oil and sugar in a mixing bowl until smooth. Add the flour, salt and baking soda and beat well. Stir in the vanilla, cinnamon, apples and pecans. Pour into a greased bundt pan. Bake at 350 degrees for 1 hour. Spoon the Topping over the hot cake. Use a knife to pull the cake from the side of the pan so the topping can seep down the edge. Let stand until cool. Invert the cake onto a serving plate. The cake will stay moist for days.

Yield: 16 servings

Topping

1 cup packed brown sugar
1/4 cup milk
1/2 cup (1 stick) margarine
1/2 teaspoon vanilla extract

Combine the brown sugar, milk, margarine and vanilla in a saucepan. Cook for 2 1/2 minutes or until smooth, stirring constantly.

Fig Preserve Cake

2 cups all-purpose flour
1 teaspoon baking soda
1 teaspoon cinnamon
1 teaspoon ground cloves
1^{1}/2 cups sugar
1 cup vegetable oil or melted butter
1 cup buttermilk
3 eggs
1 teaspoon vanilla extract
1 cup fig preserves, mashed
1 cup chopped pecans
Buttermilk Glaze (below)
Whipped cream
Ground nutmeg

Combine the flour, baking soda, cinnamon, cloves, sugar, oil, buttermilk, eggs, vanilla, preserves and pecans in a large mixing bowl and mix well. Pour into a greased and floured 9×13-inch baking pan. Bake at 350 degrees for 40 minutes or until the cake tests done. Pour the Buttermilk Glaze slowly over the hot cake. Cool. Cut into squares and arrange on serving plates. Garnish with a dollop of whipped cream and a sprinkle of nutmeg.

Yield: 15 servings

Note: You may prepare the cake up to a day or two ahead of time. Store, covered, until ready to serve. Add a little Grand Marnier to the whipped cream if desired.

Buttermilk Glaze

1 cup sugar
^{1}/2 cup (1 stick) margarine
^{1}/2 cup buttermilk
^{1}/2 teaspoon baking soda
^{1}/2 teaspoon vanilla extract

Combine the sugar, margarine, buttermilk, baking soda and vanilla in a saucepan. Bring to a boil. Boil for 4 minutes and remove from the heat.

Highlands' first post office, later Bill's Soda Shop, rang a bell when the mail carriers raced into town on horseback with the mail from Walhalla. Decades later, the sight of Mr. Mays' familiar mail truck parked in front of the post office indicated the mail's arrival.

Almond Cookies

3/4 cup sugar
1/4 cup all-purpose flour
2 1/2 cups sliced almonds

1 egg white
1/3 cup butter, melted
1 teaspoon vanilla extract

Mix the sugar, flour and almonds in a large mixing bowl. Add the egg white, butter and vanilla and mix well. Drop by tablespoonfuls onto cookie sheets lined with parchment paper. Bake at 350 degrees for 10 to 12 minutes or until golden brown. Cool on the cookie sheets. Store in an airtight container.

Yield: 2 1/2 dozen

Picnic Cookies

5 cups rolled oats
2 cups (4 sticks) butter, softened
2 cups sugar
2 cups packed brown sugar
4 eggs
2 teaspoons vanilla extract
4 cups all-purpose flour

1 teaspoon salt
2 teaspoons baking powder
2 teaspoons baking soda
4 cups (24 ounces) chocolate chips
1 (8-ounce) Hershey's candy bar, grated
3 cups chopped nuts

Process the oats in a blender to form a fine powder. Cream the butter, sugar and brown sugar in a mixing bowl until light and fluffy. Add the eggs and vanilla and beat well. Add the flour, processed oats, salt, baking powder and baking soda and beat until smooth. Stir in the chocolate chips, grated candy and nuts. Shape into balls and arrange 2 inches apart on nonstick cookie sheets. Bake at 375 degrees for 10 minutes. Cool on a wire rack.

Yield: 112 cookies

Note: You may half the recipe if desired.

Toffee Crunch Cookies

1 cup sugar
3/4 cup (1 1/2 sticks) butter, softened
1 egg
1 teaspoon vanilla extract
2 1/2 cups all-purpose flour
1 1/2 teaspoons baking powder
1/4 teaspoon baking soda
1/2 cup toffee bits or crushed Heath bars
Sugar

Combine 1 cup sugar, butter, egg and vanilla in a large mixing bowl. Beat at medium speed for 1 to 2 minutes or until creamy, scraping the bowl frequently. Add the flour, baking powder and baking soda. Beat at low speed for 1 to 2 minutes or until well mixed. Stir in the toffee bits by hand. Shape into 1 1/2-inch balls. Roll in sugar. Place two inches apart on ungreased cookie sheets. Flatten into 2 1/2-inch circles with the bottom of a glass dipped in sugar. Bake at 350 degrees for 11 to 12 minutes or until the edges just begin to turn light golden brown. Do not overbake. Cool on the cookie sheets for 1 minute. Remove to wire racks to cool completely. Sprinkle with sugar.

Yield: 2 dozen

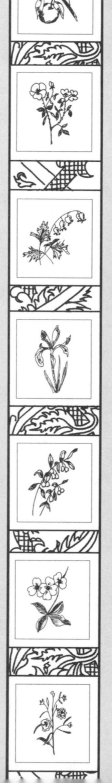

Gardening is indeed good for your health. Research conducted at the University of North Carolina at Chapel Hill shows that the health care expenditures of non-gardeners were 17.2 percent higher than those of people who garden.

After studying 3,000 women over age 50, a professor at the University of Arkansas found that the two best ways to prevent osteoporosis are gardening and weight training.

Amelia's Apricot Bars

2/3 cup dried apricots
1 cup all-purpose flour
1/2 cup (1 stick) butter, softened
1/4 cup sugar
1/3 cup all-purpose flour
1/2 teaspoon baking powder

1/4 teaspoon salt
2 eggs, beaten
1 cup packed brown sugar
1/2 teaspoon vanilla extract
1/2 cup chopped nuts
Confectioners' sugar

Rinse the apricots. Bring the apricots and water to cover to a boil in a saucepan. Boil for 10 minutes. Remove from the heat to cool. Drain and chop the apricots.

Combine 1 cup flour, butter and sugar in a bowl and mix until crumbly. Press into a greased 8×8-inch baking pan. Bake at 350 degrees for 25 minutes.

Sift 1/3 cup flour, baking powder and salt together. Beat the eggs and brown sugar in a mixing bowl until smooth. Add the flour mixture and mix well. Stir in the vanilla, nuts and apricots. Spread over the baked layer. Bake for 30 minutes or until set. Remove from the oven. Let stand untiil cool. Cut into small bars. Roll in confectioners' sugar.

Yield: 1 1/3 dozen

Note: You may double this recipe if desired.

Apple Brownies

2/3 cup butter, softened
2 cups packed brown sugar
2 eggs
1 teaspoon vanilla extract
2 cups all-purpose flour

2 teaspoons baking powder
1/4 teaspoon salt
1 cup chopped unpeeled apples
1/2 cup chopped nuts
Confectioners' sugar

Cream the butter and brown sugar in a mixing bowl until light and fluffy. Add the eggs and vanilla and mix well. Stir in the flour, baking powder and salt. Fold in the apples and nuts. Spoon into a greased 9×12-inch baking pan. Bake at 350 degrees for 30 to 35 minutes or until the brownies pull from the edges of the pan. Remove from the oven. Let stand until cool. Sprinkle with confectioners' sugar. Cut into squares.

Yield: 3 dozen

Pecan Bars

2/3 cup confectioners' sugar
2 cups all-purpose flour
1 cup (2 sticks) unsalted butter
1/2 cup honey or dark corn syrup
2/3 cup butter, melted
3 tablespoons cream
1/2 cup packed dark brown sugar
31/2 cups coarsely chopped pecans

Sift the confectioners' sugar and flour into a bowl. Cut in
1 cup butter until crumbly. Pat into a 9×12-inch baking pan.
Bake at 350 degrees for 20 minutes. Remove from the oven.

Mix the honey, 2/3 cup butter, cream and brown sugar in a
bowl until smooth. Stir in the pecans. Spread over the crust.
Bake for 25 minutes. Remove from the oven. Let stand until
cool. Cut into bars.

Yield: 3 dozen

Scotch Shortbread

1 cup (2 sticks) butter, softened
1/2 cup plus 2 tablespoons sugar
21/2 cups sifted all-purpose flour

Cream the butter in a mixing bowl until light and fluffy. Add
the sugar gradually, beating well after each addition. Add the
flour and mix well by hand. Chill, covered, in the refrigerator.
Roll the dough about 1/4 inch thick between 2 pieces of
waxed paper. Cut as desired with small cutters. Make designs
on the top of each with the tines of a fork. Arrange on an
ungreased baking sheet. Bake at 375 degrees for 20 to
25 minutes or until light golden brown. Do not overbake. Do
not substitute margarine for butter in this recipe.

Yield: 2 dozen

*When mixing
honey with other
ingredients, melt
it first in the
microwave.*

Pumpkin Bars

2 cups all-purpose flour
2 teaspoons baking powder
1 teaspoon baking soda
1 teaspoon salt
2 teaspoons cinnamon
4 eggs
1²/₃ cups sugar
1 cup vegetable oil
1 (16-ounce) can pumpkin
Cream Cheese Icing (below)

Mix the flour, baking powder, baking soda, salt and cinnamon together. Beat the eggs, sugar, oil and pumpkin in a mixing bowl until light and fluffy. Add the flour mixture and beat well. Spread in an ungreased 10×15-inch baking pan. Bake at 350 degrees for 25 to 30 minutes or until the layer tests done. Remove from the oven. Let stand until cool. Frost with Cream Cheese Icing. Cut into bars.

Yield: 4 dozen

Cream Cheese Icing

3 ounces cream cheese, softened
¹/₂ cup (1 stick) butter, softened
1 teaspoon vanilla extract
2 cups sifted confectioners' sugar

Beat the cream cheese and butter in a mixing bowl until light and fluffy. Stir in the vanilla. Add the confectioners' sugar and beat until smooth.

Yesterday is history. Tomorrow is mystery. Today is a gift. That is why it is called the present.

Cooking is like love. It should be entered into with abandon, or not at all.

128

Celebrity Chefs

&

OFF THE
MOUNTAIN

Sometimes for a change, we like to go off the mountain. In early April when our landscape is still in winter's grip, we seek out a preview of spring by dipping down into the valleys of Rabun County or Cullasaja along the River. Here trees are cloaked in the tender greens and pinks of spring when our limbs are only black branches…

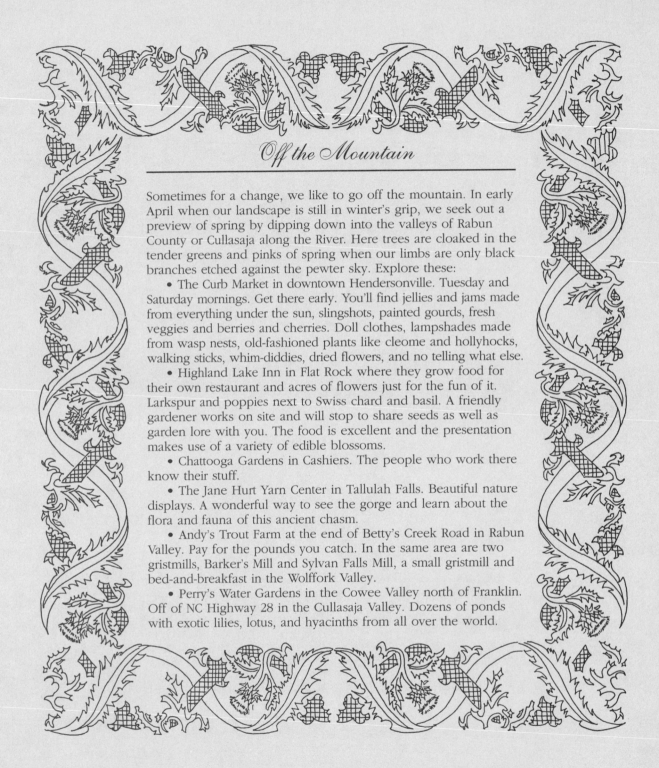

Off the Mountain

Sometimes for a change, we like to go off the mountain. In early April when our landscape is still in winter's grip, we seek out a preview of spring by dipping down into the valleys of Rabun County or Cullasaja along the River. Here trees are cloaked in the tender greens and pinks of spring when our limbs are only black branches etched against the pewter sky. Explore these:

• The Curb Market in downtown Hendersonville. Tuesday and Saturday mornings. Get there early. You'll find jellies and jams made from everything under the sun, slingshots, painted gourds, fresh veggies and berries and cherries. Doll clothes, lampshades made from wasp nests, old-fashioned plants like cleome and hollyhocks, walking sticks, whim-diddies, dried flowers, and no telling what else.

• Highland Lake Inn in Flat Rock where they grow food for their own restaurant and acres of flowers just for the fun of it. Larkspur and poppies next to Swiss chard and basil. A friendly gardener works on site and will stop to share seeds as well as garden lore with you. The food is excellent and the presentation makes use of a variety of edible blossoms.

• Chattooga Gardens in Cashiers. The people who work there know their stuff.

• The Jane Hurt Yarn Center in Tallulah Falls. Beautiful nature displays. A wonderful way to see the gorge and learn about the flora and fauna of this ancient chasm.

• Andy's Trout Farm at the end of Betty's Creek Road in Rabun Valley. Pay for the pounds you catch. In the same area are two gristmills, Barker's Mill and Sylvan Falls Mill, a small gristmill and bed-and-breakfast in the Wolffork Valley.

• Perry's Water Gardens in the Cowee Valley north of Franklin. Off of NC Highway 28 in the Cullasaja Valley. Dozens of ponds with exotic lilies, lotus, and hyacinths from all over the world.

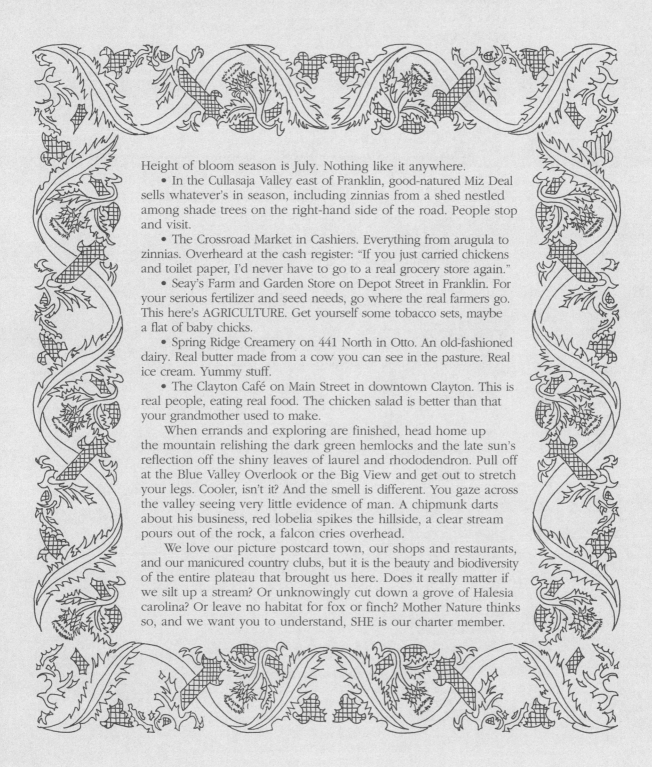

Height of bloom season is July. Nothing like it anywhere.

• In the Cullasaja Valley east of Franklin, good-natured Miz Deal sells whatever's in season, including zinnias from a shed nestled among shade trees on the right-hand side of the road. People stop and visit.

• The Crossroad Market in Cashiers. Everything from arugula to zinnias. Overheard at the cash register: "If you just carried chickens and toilet paper, I'd never have to go to a real grocery store again."

• Seay's Farm and Garden Store on Depot Street in Franklin. For your serious fertilizer and seed needs, go where the real farmers go. This here's AGRICULTURE. Get yourself some tobacco sets, maybe a flat of baby chicks.

• Spring Ridge Creamery on 441 North in Otto. An old-fashioned dairy. Real butter made from a cow you can see in the pasture. Real ice cream. Yummy stuff.

• The Clayton Café on Main Street in downtown Clayton. This is real people, eating real food. The chicken salad is better than that your grandmother used to make.

When errands and exploring are finished, head home up the mountain relishing the dark green hemlocks and the late sun's reflection off the shiny leaves of laurel and rhododendron. Pull off at the Blue Valley Overlook or the Big View and get out to stretch your legs. Cooler, isn't it? And the smell is different. You gaze across the valley seeing very little evidence of man. A chipmunk darts about his business, red lobelia spikes the hillside, a clear stream pours out of the rock, a falcon cries overhead.

We love our picture postcard town, our shops and restaurants, and our manicured country clubs, but it is the beauty and biodiversity of the entire plateau that brought us here. Does it really matter if we silt up a stream? Or unknowingly cut down a grove of Halesia carolina? Or leave no habitat for fox or finch? Mother Nature thinks so, and we want you to understand, SHE is our charter member.

Breakfast Oysters

1/4 cup chopped green onions
1/4 cup minced parsley
1 teaspoon Tabasco sauce
1 cup (2 sticks) butter
2 pints Pacific oysters, drained, shells reserved
Freshly ground pepper to taste
1 lemon, cut into halves
5 slices bacon, cooked, crumbled
8 slices bread, cut into points or circles, toasted, or
    saltines

Sauté the green onions, parsley and Tabasco sauce in the butter in a skillet until the green onions are soft. Arrange the oysters on oyster shells in a single layer in a broiler pan. Pour the sautéed mixture over the top. Sprinkle the oysters with pepper until coated. Broil for 2$1/2$ minutes. Squeeze the lemon over the oysters. Broil for 3 minutes longer or until the oysters begin to curl. Sprinkle with the crumbled bacon. Spoon over the toasted bread on serving plates.

Yield: 8 servings

ANN BAIRD

All that is required of a great houseguest is that he amuse himself by day and his host and hostess by night.

Bleu Cheese Torte with Sun-Dried Tomatoes and Pesto

2 ounces sun-dried tomatoes
2 tablespoons olive oil
1 pound cream cheese, softened
8 ounces bleu cheese, crumbled
1 1/2 cups fresh spinach
1/2 cup chopped fresh parsley
1 cup fresh basil leaves
1 garlic clove, minced
2 tablespoons grated Parmesan cheese
2 tablespoons olive oil

Reconstitute the sun-dried tomatoes in warm water and drain. Purée the sun-dried tomatoes with 2 tablespoons olive oil in a food processor. Spoon into a bowl. Process the cream cheese and bleu cheese in a food processor until smooth. Spoon into a bowl. Purée the spinach, parsley, basil, garlic, Parmesan cheese and 2 tablespoons olive oil in a food processor until smooth.

Line a large loaf pan with plastic wrap, leaving a 6-inch overhang on each end. Spread 1/4 of the cheese mixture over the bottom of the pan. Layer the sun-dried tomato purée over the cheese. Spread 1/3 of the remaining cheese over the sun-dried tomato layer, using a wet spoon to smooth. Layer the pesto and the remaining cheese mixture over the top. Tap the pan on the counter to remove any air bubbles. Cover with the plastic wrap. Chill for 3 to 12 hours before serving. Unwrap and invert onto a serving plate. Serve with French bread or crackers.

Yield: 30 servings

WILD THYME RESTAURANT
NANCY AND CARTER BRUNS

Central House Meat Loaf

1/2 red onion, coarsely chopped
1/2 green bell pepper, coarsely chopped
2 pounds ground beef
1 1/2 cups bread crumbs
2 eggs
1 garlic clove, chopped
1/4 cup pickle relish
1/4 cup ketchup
3 tablespoons Worcestershire sauce
1 teaspoon salt
1/2 teaspoon black pepper
1/2 teaspoon lemon pepper
Meat Loaf Glaze (below)

Purée the onion and bell pepper in a food processor. Combine with the ground beef, bread crumbs, eggs, garlic, pickle relish, ketchup, Worcestershire sauce, salt, black pepper and lemon pepper in a large bowl and mix well. Shape into a loaf and place in a 5×9-inch loaf pan. Bake at 350 degrees for 45 minutes. Spread the Meat Loaf Glaze over the top. Bake for 20 minutes longer or until the meat loaf is cooked through.

Yield: 8 servings

Meat Loaf Glaze

1/2 cup ketchup
2 tablespoons brown sugar
2 teaspoons Worcestershire sauce

Combine the ketchup, brown sugar and Worcestershire sauce in a small bowl and mix well.

CENTRAL HOUSE RESTAURANT

Central House's reputation for good food is as old as its beginning. Louis Edwards remembers when he was a boy: "My job was to catch and kill the chickens for dinner. They were doused in boiling water so feathers could be removed before they were cleaned. Many a chicken ended up on the Central House table in less than an hour of the time when it was well and running around the chicken yard."

Corn-for-Breakfast Casserole

6 ounces grated Monterey Jack
  cheese
2 cups frozen whole kernel corn
9 eggs
1/2 teaspoon salt

1/4 teaspoon black pepper
1/4 teaspoon nutmeg
Dash of cayenne pepper
1 1/2 cups skim milk
3/4 cup half-and-half

Layer the cheese and corn 1/2 at a time in a greased 9×13-inch baking dish.
Beat the eggs in a mixing bowl. Season with the salt, black pepper, nutmeg and
cayenne pepper. Add the milk and half-and-half and beat well. Pour over the
layers. Bake, uncovered, at 325 degrees for 1 hour or until puffy and light brown.

Yield: 6 servings

COLONIAL PINES INN
DONNA ALLEY

Applesauce Cake

1 1/2 cups applesauce
1 cup (2 sticks) margarine
1 teaspoon cinnamon
1 teaspoon ground cloves
1/2 teaspoon nutmeg
2 cups all-purpose flour

2 teaspoons baking soda
2 teaspoons baking powder
1 cup sugar
3 tablespoons baking cocoa
1 cup chopped nuts
1 cup raisins

Heat the applesauce and margarine in a saucepan until the margarine melts,
stirring frequently. Add the cinnamon, cloves and nutmeg and mix well. Sift the
flour, baking soda, baking powder, sugar and baking cocoa into a large bowl.
Stir in the nuts and raisins. Add the applesauce mixture and mix well. Spoon
into a greased 9×13-inch cake pan. Bake at 350 degrees for 30 minutes or until
the cake tests done.

Yield: 15 servings

ISABEL CHAMBERS

Marie's Chilled Cherry Soup

3 cups water
3/4 cup sugar
1 cinnamon stick
Zest of 1 orange
4 cups pitted fresh tart cherries
1 tablespoon arrowroot or cornstarch
1/3 cup cream
1/2 cup dry red wine

Combine the water, sugar, cinnamon stick and orange zest in a saucepan. Bring to a boil. Add the cherries and reduce the heat. Simmer for 30 minutes. Remove the cinnamon stick. Mix the arrowroot with 2 tablespoons of the cherry mixture in a small bowl. Return to the saucepan. Return to a boil and reduce the heat, stirring constantly. Simmer for 30 minutes or until slightly thickened. Spoon into a large heatproof bowl. Chill, covered, in the refrigerator. The mixture will thicken as it cools. To serve, stir in the cream and wine. Ladle into Champagne or wine glasses to show off the color. Garnish with cinnamon sticks and/or a dollop of sour cream or yogurt.

Yield: 8 servings

CULLASAJA COUNTRY CLUB

Fudge Pie

2 squares unsweetened baking chocolate
1/2 cup (1 stick) butter
2 eggs, beaten
1 cup sugar
1/4 cup all-purpose flour
1 unbaked (8-inch) pie shell

Melt the chocolate and butter in a small saucepan. Combine the eggs, sugar and flour in a mixing bowl and mix well. Stir in the chocolate mixture. Pour into the pie shell. Bake at 350 degrees for 20 to 25 minutes or until the center of the pie is slightly shaky. Cut into wedges while still warm. Cool completely before serving. Serve with ice cream.

Yield: 6 to 8 servings

FIRESIDE INN RESTAURANT

Garlic Bean Soup

1 pound dried baby lima beans
4 garlic cloves, pressed
1/2 cup chopped onion
Salt and pepper to taste
Olive oil
1 large or 2 small onions, chopped
2 carrots, chopped
2 tablespoons chopped garlic
8 cups vegetable broth
Texas Pete sauce to taste
Tamari to taste

Sort and rinse the lima beans. Soak the beans in water to cover in a bowl for 8 to 12 hours; drain and rinse. Place the beans in a saucepan. Add enough water to cover the beans by 4 inches. Bring to a boil and reduce the heat, skimming the surface. Add the pressed garlic and 1/2 cup onion. Cook until the beans are tender, adding additional water or vegetable stock as needed and skimming the surface. Season with salt and pepper.

Add enough olive oil to a large stockpot to coat the bottom. Add the chopped onions. Sauté until slightly caramelized. Add the carrots and chopped garlic. Sauté until tender. Add the beans and vegetable broth. Bring to a boil and reduce the heat. Simmer until the flavors are blended. Season with Texas Pete sauce, tamari, salt and pepper.

Yield: 8 servings

Note: You may add fresh or frozen chopped greens, such as spinach or collards.

**FRESSERS EATERY
DEBBIE GROSSMAN**

Get in the habit of roasting a couple of heads of garlic and storing them tightly covered in the refrigerator. The roasted garlic can be added to mashed potatoes or vegetables, or spread on toasted bread. Roasted garlic also acts as a thickening agent when added to sauces and gravies. When whisked, it will thicken an oil and vinegar dressing, as well.

Lemon Biscotti

2 eggs
1/2 cup sugar
1/2 cup vegetable oil

2 teaspoons baking powder
2 teaspoons lemon extract
2 1/2 cups all-purpose flour

Combine the eggs, sugar, oil, baking powder, lemon extract and flour in a large bowl and mix well to form a stiff dough. Break into small pieces. Roll each piece on a floured surface until 2 to 2 1/2 inches long. Shape into an "S" shape. Arrange on nonstick cookie sheets. Bake at 350 to 375 degrees until golden brown. Cool on wire racks. Store in an airtight container.

Yield: 2 dozen

THE GASLIGHT CAFÉ
JOANN GUNIO

Eggplant Soup

1/2 cup (1 stick) unsalted butter
3/4 cup finely chopped onion
3/4 cup finely chopped celery
1 1/2 cups 1/2-inch cubes peeled
　red potato
2 1/2 cups 1/2-inch cubes peeled
　eggplant

1/8 tablespoon curry powder
1/2 tablespoon thyme
1/2 tablespoon sweet basil
4 cups chicken stock
2 cups heavy cream
4 green onions, thinly sliced

Melt the butter in a heavy stockpot. Add the onion, celery, potato and eggplant. Season with the curry powder, thyme and basil. Sauté until the potatoes begin to stick to the stockpot. Add the chicken stock. Bring to a boil and reduce the heat. Simmer until thickened, stirring frequently. Remove from the heat. Stir in the cream. Ladle into soup bowls. Sprinkle with the green onions.

Yield: 8 servings

Note: Remember, as for any soup, a good stock is most important.

WOLFGANGS ON MAIN
WOLFGANG GREEN

Grillades and Grits

3 pounds beef shoulder or round, cut into serving pieces
1/2 cup vegetable oil
1/2 cup all-purpose flour
1 cup chopped green bell pepper
1 cup chopped onion
1 cup chopped celery
1 teaspoon minced garlic
1 cup crushed fresh or canned tomatoes
2 bay leaves
2 cups beef broth
1 cup red wine
1/2 tablespoon salt
1/2 teaspoon cayenne pepper
1/2 teaspoon white pepper
1/2 teaspoon black pepper
1/2 teaspoon thyme
1/2 teaspoon paprika
1/2 teaspoon dry mustard
Hot cooked grits

Brown the beef in batches in 1/4 cup of the oil in a skillet. Remove to a warm platter. Add the remaining 1/4 cup oil to the skillet. Stir in the flour. Heat to form a medium to dark roux, whisking constantly. Add the bell pepper, onion, celery and garlic. Sauté until light brown. Reduce the heat to medium. Add the tomatoes, bay leaves, beef broth and red wine, stirring well after each addition. Return the beef to the skillet. Season with salt, cayenne pepper, white pepper, black pepper, thyme, paprika and dry mustard. Simmer for 2 hours or until thickened to a thick gravy consistency, stirring occasionally. Discard the bay leaves. Serve over hot cooked grits.

Yield: 10 servings

Note: You may freeze this recipe, and water may be added after thawing.

WINSTON GROOM, AUTHOR OF *FORREST GUMP*, AND ANNE-CLINTON GROOM

The hostess must be like the duck: calm and unruffled on the surface and paddling like hell underneath.

—Anonymous

Mushroom Croustades

24 thin slices white bread
2 tablespoons butter, softened
3 tablespoons minced shallots
$1/4$ cup ($1/2$ stick) butter
8 ounces fresh mushrooms, finely chopped
2 tablespoons all-purpose flour
1 cup heavy cream
$1^1/2$ tablespoons minced chives
1 tablespoon minced parsley
$1/2$ teaspoon lemon juice
$1/2$ teaspoon salt
$1/8$ teaspoon cayenne pepper
2 tablespoons freshly grated Parmesan cheese
2 teaspoons minced parsley
Butter

Cut a 3-inch round from each bread slice. Brush the insides of miniature muffin cups with 2 tablespoons butter. Fit the bread rounds gently into each prepared muffin cup to form a cup. Bake at 400 degrees for 10 minutes or until light brown. Remove from the oven to cool.

Sauté the shallots in $1/4$ cup butter in a heavy skillet for 1 minute. Stir in the mushrooms. Simmer, uncovered, for 10 minutes or until all of the liquid is evaporated. Remove from the heat. Stir in the flour. Pour the cream over the top. Return to the heat and bring to a boil, stirring constantly. Cook for 1 minute longer or until thickened, stirring constantly. Remove from the heat. Stir in the chives, parsley, lemon juice, salt and cayenne pepper. Let stand until cool. Chill, covered, in the refrigerator.

Spoon the mushroom mixture into the toasted bread shells in the miniature muffin cups. Freeze in the muffin cups. Remove from the muffin cups. Place in sealable plastic freezer bags and seal the bags. Store in the freezer until needed.

To serve, thaw the croustades completely before baking. Arrange on ungreased baking sheets. Sprinkle with Parmesan cheese and parsley. Dot with butter. Bake at 350 degrees for 10 minutes. Broil until brown. Serve immediately.

Yield: 2 dozen

CHUCK HAMMOCK

Grilled Salmon with Nasturtium Butter

2 cups (4 sticks) unsalted
  butter, softened
2 tablespoons chopped
  fresh tarragon
6 tablespoons chopped
  nasturtiums (6 to
  10 flowers)

3 tablespoons lemon juice
1 shallot, finely chopped
1 teaspoon freshly ground
  pepper
1 teaspoon sea salt
2 (6-ounce) salmon fillets

Beat the butter in a small bowl until smooth and creamy.
Add the tarragon, nasturtiums, lemon juice, shallot, pepper
and sea salt and mix well. Add additional lemon juice if
needed for the desired consistency. Adjust the seasonings.
Shape into logs and wrap in waxed paper. Chill until firm.
Slice into medallions. Grill the salmon over hot coals until the
salmon flakes easily. Arrange on serving plates. Top each with
nasturtium butter medallions. Garnish with fresh nasturtiums.

Yield: 2 servings

HIGHLANDS COUNTRY CLUB
MARK BARNETT

Boule de Neigh

2 cups (4 sticks) butter
1 pound bitter or
  semisweet chocolate
1 pound sugar (2¼ cups)

1 cup boiling coffee or
  water
8 eggs, beaten
1½ tablespoons Grand
  Marnier

Melt the butter, chocolate and sugar in a double boiler over
hot water. Stir in the coffee. Add a small amount of the chocolate
mixture to the beaten eggs. Add the eggs to the chocolate
mixture and beat well. Stir in the Grand Marnier. Pour into a
lined 10-inch torte pan. Bake at 350 degrees until the torte rises
and falls a little with a leather-like top. Cut into small wedges.

Yield: 8 servings

HIGHLANDS FALLS COUNTRY CLUB

*Nasturtiums, which
grow well in our
cool weather, may
be used in many
ways: The peppery
leaves are great
in salads or
sandwiches, the
flowers add both
decoration and
nutrition to salads,
and the immature
seeds and buds
become the capers
that we use to perk
up cold salmon
and potato salad.
In addition to
nasturtiums, other
edible flowers that
may be used to
decorate a soft
cheese mold or a
wedding cake or
perk up a garden
salad or garnish
a fruit dessert are
daylilies (especially
the buds), squash,
violets, pansies,
lilacs, roses, and
marigolds.*

Greek Spaghetti

1 medium onion, chopped
1 green bell pepper, chopped
1/2 cup (1 stick) butter or margarine
1 (4-ounce) can mushroom stems and pieces, drained
1 (4-ounce) can chopped black olives, drained
1 (28-ounce) can diced tomatoes
12 ounces spaghetti, cooked, drained
8 ounces sharp Cheddar cheese, shredded
1 (10-ounce) can mushroom soup
1/4 cup water

Sauté the onion and bell pepper in the butter in a skillet until soft. Add the mushrooms and olives. Sauté for 5 minutes. Add the tomatoes. Simmer for 10 minutes. Layer the spaghetti and tomato mixture 1/2 at a time in a 9×13-inch baking dish sprayed with nonstick cooking spray. Sprinkle with the cheese. Mix the mushroom soup and water in a bowl. Pour over the layers. Bake at 350 degrees for 30 minutes or until bubbly.

Yield: 8 to 10 servings

REVEREND MIKE JONES

Mountain Corn Chowder

1/4 cup chopped sliced bacon
3 cups fresh Silver Queen corn
1/4 cup chopped Vidalia onion
2 cups chicken stock
2 cups heavy cream
1/4 cup sweet sherry
1 teaspoon cumin
1 teaspoon coriander
1 teaspoon chopped garlic
1 tablespoon sugar
1 teaspoon salt
1/2 teaspoon pepper
2 tablespoons cornstarch
1/2 cup water

Cook the bacon in a skillet until crisp and crumbly. Drain the bacon, reserving the bacon drippings. Sauté the corn and onion in the reserved bacon drippings in a large stockpot over medium heat until the onion is soft. Add the chicken stock, cream and sherry. Simmer for 10 minutes. Stir in the cumin, coriander, garlic, sugar, salt and pepper. Cook over low heat for 20 minutes. Mix the cornstarch with the water. Add to the chowder. Cook until thickened, stirring constantly. Ladle into soup bowls. Sprinkle with the bacon.

Yield: 8 servings

THE KELSEY PLACE RESTAURANT

Shrimp and Cheese in Puff Pastry with Orange Curry Sauce

2 eggs
2 to 3 teaspoons water
2 sheets puff pastry, cut
   into triangles
2 pounds jumbo shrimp,
   peeled, deveined,
   butterflied

8 ounces provolone or
   smoked Gouda cheese,
   cut into 1/4-inch slices
Orange Curry Sauce
   (below)

Beat the eggs with the water in a small bowl. Brush the pastry triangles with the egg mixture. Stuff the shrimp with the cheese. Place the stuffed shrimp in the center of each pastry. Fold the pastry over the shrimp to enclose, pressing the edges to seal. Arrange seam side down on greased baking sheets. Brush with the egg mixture. Bake at 375 degrees for 15 to 20 minutes or until golden brown. Serve with Orange Curry Sauce.

Yield: 10 to 12 servings

Orange Curry Sauce

3 cups orange juice
1 tablespoon curry powder
1/4 cup sugar

3 tablespoons cornstarch
1 cup water

Heat the orange juice, curry powder and sugar in a saucepan until the sugar dissolves, stirring frequently. Mix the cornstarch and water in a bowl. Stir into the orange juice mixture gradually. Cook until thickened, stirring constantly.

THE LOG CABIN STEAK HOUSE
HAROLD LEE

Watch your neighbor's corn patch. About twenty days after the silks appear, corn will be ready for harvest.

In high summer when fresh corn is in season, eat it at every meal. Buy it at Shorty's roadside stand on Highway 106 south of downtown Scaly Mountain. Ask for some she's "pulled" that morning.

Cheddar Chili Cheesecake

1¹/₂ tablespoons butter
¹/₄ cup fine bread crumbs
¹/₄ cup shredded Cheddar cheese
6 ounces thinly sliced ham
1¹/₂ pounds cream cheese, softened
12 ounces sharp Cheddar cheese, shredded
1 cup cottage cheese
³/₄ cup chopped green onions
4 eggs
3 tablespoons finely chopped seeded jalapeños
2 tablespoons milk
1 garlic clove, minced

Spread the butter in a 9-inch springform pan. Mix the bread crumbs and ¹/₄ cup Cheddar cheese in a bowl. Sprinkle into the prepared pan, turning to coat. Chill, covered, in the refrigerator.

Chop ¹/₂ of the ham. Process the chopped ham, cream cheese, 12 ounces Cheddar cheese, cottage cheese, green onions, eggs, chiles, milk and garlic in a food processor until smooth. Pour slightly more than half of the filling into the prepared pan. Arrange the remaining thinly sliced ham in an even layer over the filling. Cover with the remaining filling. Set the springform pan on a baking sheet. Bake at 325 degrees for 1¹/₄ hours. Turn off the oven and leave the oven door ajar. Let the cheesecake cool in the oven for 1 hour. Remove the cheesecake to a wire rack. Remove the side of the pan. Cool to room temperature before serving.

Yield: 12 to 15 servings

> ### LET HOLLY DO THE COOKING
> ### HOLLY MATHIOWDIS

Sharing a division or a cutting of a favorite plant is like taking out garden insurance: If your plant fails for some reason, but the shared plant survives, all is not lost; your friend will surely give you back a start.

ASOA Salad

ASOA means Almonds, Spinach, Oranges, Avocado (or "Add Something Or Another") since most of my recipes are created as I go.

1/2 cup honey
1/2 cup Dijon mustard
1/3 cup vegetable oil
1/4 cup white wine vinegar
1/4 cup orange juice
1 tablespoon grated onion
1 teaspoon salt
Zest of 6 oranges

2/3 cup sliced almonds
Butter
1 (10-ounce) package baby spinach
2 (10-ounce) packages baby greens
   or spring mix
Sections of 6 oranges
2 avocados, sliced

Microwave the honey in a microwave-safe dish until melted. Add the Dijon mustard and mix well. Stir in the oil, white wine vinegar, orange juice, onion, salt and orange zest. Toss the almonds in butter in a baking pan. Bake at 350 degrees until brown and toasted. Combine the spinach, baby greens, oranges, avocados and toasted almonds in a large salad bowl and toss to mix. Add the dressing and toss.

Yield: 8 servings

JILL MONTANA

Shrimp and Artichoke Casserole

8 ounces sliced mushrooms
1/2 cup (1 stick) butter
1 pound shrimp, cooked
1 (14-ounce) can artichoke hearts,
   drained, cut into quarters
41/2 tablespoons all-purpose flour
3/4 cup milk

3/4 cup heavy cream
1/2 cup dry sherry
1 tablespoon Worcestershire sauce
1 teaspoon salt
1/8 teaspoon pepper
1/2 cup grated Parmesan cheese
Paprika to taste

Sauté the mushrooms in 21/2 tablespoons of the butter in a skillet. Layer the shrimp, mushrooms and artichokes in a greased 2-quart baking dish. Melt the remaining butter in a saucepan. Add the flour, milk and cream. Cook until thickened, whisking constantly. Add the sherry, Worcestershire sauce, salt and pepper. Pour over the layers. Chill, covered, for 24 hours if desired. Sprinkle with Parmesan cheese and paprika. Bake at 375 degrees for 30 minutes. Serve over rice.

Yield: 8 servings

JOHN NEWSOME

145

On The Verandah's Crabcakes

1/2 cup minced red onion
1/2 cup minced celery
1/2 cup minced red bell pepper
1/2 cup (1 stick) butter, melted
1 1/2 cups dry bread crumbs
1 tablespoon Alan's Maniac
    Jalapeño Sauce
1/4 teaspoon black pepper
1/8 teaspoon cayenne pepper
2 tablespoons chopped parsley
Salt to taste

6 ounces rock shrimp, peeled,
    deveined, chopped
6 ounces surimi, finely chopped
8 ounces lump crab meat
2 eggs, beaten
1/3 cup heavy cream
Vegetable oil for frying
Alan's Maniac Carib Spicy Mango
    Salsa (page 147)
On The Verandah's Daikon Pepper
    Slaw (below)

Sauté the onion, celery and bell pepper in the butter in a sauté pan for about 5 minutes. Remove from the heat. Add the bread crumbs and mix well. Stir in the Alan's Maniac Jalapeño Sauce, black pepper, cayenne pepper, parsley and salt. Fold in the rock shrimp, surimi and crab meat. Beat the eggs and cream in a bowl. Add to the seafood mixture and mix well. Shape into 3-inch patties. Fry in hot oil in a skillet until golden brown and cooked through. Serve with Alan's Maniac Carib Spicy Mango Salsa and On The Verandah's Daikon Pepper Slaw.

Yield: 15 crabcakes

On The Verandah's Daikon Pepper Slaw

2 cups shredded daikon radish
2 cups julienned red bell pepper
2 cups julienned yellow bell pepper
1 cup shredded green onion tops
1/4 cup shredded carrot
2 tablespoons rice wine vinegar
2 tablespoons fresh lime juice

6 tablespoons peanut oil
2 tablespoons ajipon citrus
    soy sauce
2 tablespoons mirin seasoning
1/2 teaspoon Alan's Maniac Liming
    Sauce
Salt and pepper to taste

Combine the radish, bell peppers, green onion tops and carrot in a large bowl and toss to mix. Combine the rice wine vinegar, lime juice, peanut oil, ajipon citrus soy sauce, mirin seasoning, Alan's Maniac Liming Sauce, salt and pepper in a bowl and mix well. Pour over the vegetable mixture and toss to coat.

Alan's Maniac Carib Spicy Mango Salsa

4 cups chopped fresh
  mango
2 tablespoons Alan's
  Maniac Carib Sauce

1/4 cup fresh lime juice
1/2 teaspoon white pepper
Salt to taste

Combine the mango, Alan's Maniac Carib Sauce, lime juice, white pepper and salt in a bowl and mix well.

ON THE VERANDAH

Risotto ai Funghi Porcini

12 ounces fresh porcini
  mushrooms, sliced
2 teaspoons minced garlic
1/4 bunch flat-leaf Italian
  parsley, chopped
2 tablespoons extra-virgin
  olive oil
1 medium onion, chopped
2 tablespoons extra-virgin
  olive oil

2 1/2 cups uncooked
  arborio rice
3/4 cup white wine
3 cups boiling chicken
  stock
Salt and pepper to taste
1/3 cup grated Parmigiano-
  Reggiano
1 teaspoon truffle oil

Sauté the mushrooms, garlic and parsley in 2 tablespoons olive oil in a skillet until tender. Sauté the onion in 2 tablespoons olive oil in a skillet until translucent. Add the rice. Sauté for 1 minute. Stir in the white wine. Add 1 ladle of the boiling chicken stock. Cook until the liquid is absorbed, stirring constantly. Repeat until the rice is creamy. Total cooking time will be about 15 minutes. Remove from the heat. Add the sautéed mushrooms, salt and pepper and mix well. Add the Parmigiano-Reggiano and toss to mix. Drizzle with the truffle oil. Serve immediately.

Yield: 8 servings

PAOLETTI'S RESTAURANT

When you are invited to a dinner party in Highlands, remember there is no such thing as "fashionably late." We always arrive promptly at the appointed hour.

Tomato Florentine Soup

1½ large onions, chopped
¼ cup garlic, minced
½ cup olive oil
3 tablespoons dried basil
2 tablespoons Italian seasoning
2 bay leaves
Salt and pepper to taste
3 tablespoons celery salt
1 cup white wine
1 (48-ounce) can vegetable juice cocktail
1 pound roux
½ cup sugar
1½ quarts heavy cream
8 pounds tomatoes, chopped
1 gallon milk
1 pound fresh spinach, chopped
4 ounces fresh basil, chopped

Sauté the onions and garlic in the olive oil in a stockpot for 6 minutes. Add the dried basil, Italian seasoning, bay leaves, salt, pepper, celery salt and white wine. Cook for 5 minutes. Add the vegetable juice cocktail. Boil for 3 minutes. Add the roux. Cook until thickened, stirring constantly. Add the sugar, cream, tomatoes and milk. Simmer for 15 minutes. Add the spinach and fresh basil and mix well. Adjust the seasonings with salt and pepper. Discard the bay leaves before serving.

Yield: 2 gallons

LAKESIDE RESTAURANT
MARTY ROSENFIELD

Mix your own birdseed by buying the materials from The Bird Barn or a feed store like Seay's in Franklin. A great mix includes 25 pounds of black oil sunflower seeds, 10 pounds of white proso millet, 10 pounds of cracked corn, and maybe some sunflower hearts. Store in a large rodent-proof container. DO NOT LEAVE IT ON YOUR DECK. NO CONTAINER IS BEAR PROOF.

1/2 cup olive oil
11/2 pounds lamb leg or shoulder meat
Salt and black pepper to taste
3 onions, chopped
2 to 3 tablespoons cumin
2 teaspoons cinnamon
4 pounds tomatoes, chopped or crushed
1 quart chicken stock
1 quart veal or beef stock
3 or 4 bay leaves
1 tablespoon fresh thyme
1 large eggplant, peeled, cubed
4 potatoes, cubed
1 large butternut squash, peeled, cubed
1 quart garbanzo beans, drained, rinsed
1/2 cup honey
2 to 4 zucchini or yellow squash, chopped
2 red bell peppers, coarsely chopped
Cayenne pepper to taste

Heat the olive oil in a Dutch oven. Cut the lamb into cubes. Season with salt and black pepper. Sauté the lamb in the oil in batches until all of the lamb is seared, removing each batch to a plate with a slotted spoon. Add the onions to the pan drippings. Sauté until tender. Add the cumin and cinnamon. Stir in the tomatoes, chicken stock, veal stock, bay leaves and thyme. Return the lamb to the Dutch oven. Bake, covered, at 375 degrees for 30 minutes. Add the eggplant, potatoes, butternut squash and garbanzo beans and mix well. Cook for 30 minutes. Stir in the honey. Add the zucchini and bell peppers and mix well. Bake, uncovered, for 15 minutes. Season with salt, black pepper and cayenne pepper. Discard the bay leaves. Serve hot over polenta.

Yield: 12 to 16 servings

Note: To bake in a convection oven, decrease the temperature by 25 degrees and the baking time by 5 to 10 minutes. Also, you may use whatever vegetables are in season.

ROSEWOOD MARKET
TIM LUNDY

Chocolate Cream Pots

6 tablespoons sugar
2 cups heavy cream
4 ounces extra-bittersweet chocolate
1/4 cup coffee liqueur
4 egg yolks, at room temperature
Pinch of salt

Heat the sugar in a saucepan until caramelized, stirring constantly. Divide between six 4-ounce ramekins. Place the ramekins in a 9×9-inch or 8×12-inch baking pan. Heat the cream in a small saucepan. Add the chocolate and liqueur. Heat until smooth, stirring constantly. Do not boil. Whip the egg yolks and salt in a small bowl. Add 1/2 cup of the chocolate cream in a steady stream, beating constantly. Add the egg yolk mixture gradually to the remaining chocolate cream, stirring constantly. Pour into the prepared ramekins. Pour enough boiling water into the baking pan to come halfway up the side of the ramekins. Bake at 325 degrees for 40 to 45 minutes or until set. Remove from the oven to cool. Chill, covered, until ready to serve. To serve, set the ramekins in a pan of hot water for a few minutes. Invert onto serving plates. Garnish with fresh fruit and whipped cream.

Yield: 6 servings

SKYLINE LODGE RESTAURANT
JACK ADRIAN

Highlands Apples in a Dish

6 medium apples
1/4 cup sugar
1/2 lemon, seeded, ground
8 slices white bread
1 cup (2 sticks) margarine, melted
1 cup (or more) packed light brown sugar

Peel and core the apples. Cut into quarters. Combine the apples, sugar and lemon in a saucepan. Bring just to the boiling point. Remove from the heat and cover. Let stand for 1 hour; drain. Place the apples in a 2 1/2-quart baking dish.

Trim the crusts from the bread. Cut each bread slice into 4 squares. Pour 1/2 of the margarine into a small bowl. Place the brown sugar in a shallow dish. Dip a bread square in the margarine and then in the brown sugar to coat both sides. Stand the square up on the apple layer against the rim of the baking dish. Repeat with the second bread square, overlapping 2/3 of the first square. Repeat until all of the bread squares, margarine and brown sugar are used and the apples are covered with overlapping squares. Bake at 275 degrees for 1 hour.

Yield: 8 servings

MARY THOMPSON

Sign in a Highlands shop: "Unattended children will be given a free kitten."

Shrimp and Eggplant Casserole

2 pounds shrimp, peeled, deveined
1/4 cup vegetable oil
1 medium onion, chopped
1 cup finely chopped celery
1 medium bell pepper, chopped
2 eggplant, peeled, cut into cubes
Salt to taste
Red pepper and garlic to taste
2 cups slightly undercooked rice
1 (10-ounce) can cream of mushroom soup
8 ounces sharp Cheddar cheese, grated
Buttered toasted bread crumbs
Paprika to taste

Fry the shrimp in the oil in a heavy cast-iron skillet over medium heat until the shrimp turn pink, stirring gently. Remove the shrimp from the skillet to a heated large bowl. Add the onion, celery and bell pepper. Sauté until tender-crisp. Add to the shrimp.

Place the eggplant in a saucepan. Cover with lightly salted water. Simmer until tender but not too soft; drain. Season with red pepper, garlic and salt. Add the eggplant and rice to the shrimp mixture and stir lightly. Spoon into a 2¹/₂-quart baking dish. Pour the soup over the top. Sprinkle with the cheese, bread crumbs and paprika. Bake at 350 degrees for 25 minutes.

Yield: 8 servings

JONATHAN WILLIAMS
PUBLISHER OF
WHITE TRASH COOKING

Use different colored bandanas as napkins at your next outdoor meal. After the meal your guests can tie them around their necks bandana style, or over their hair, or bind up imaginary wounds, wrap up a leftover piece of pie, or cover their faces and take a nap.

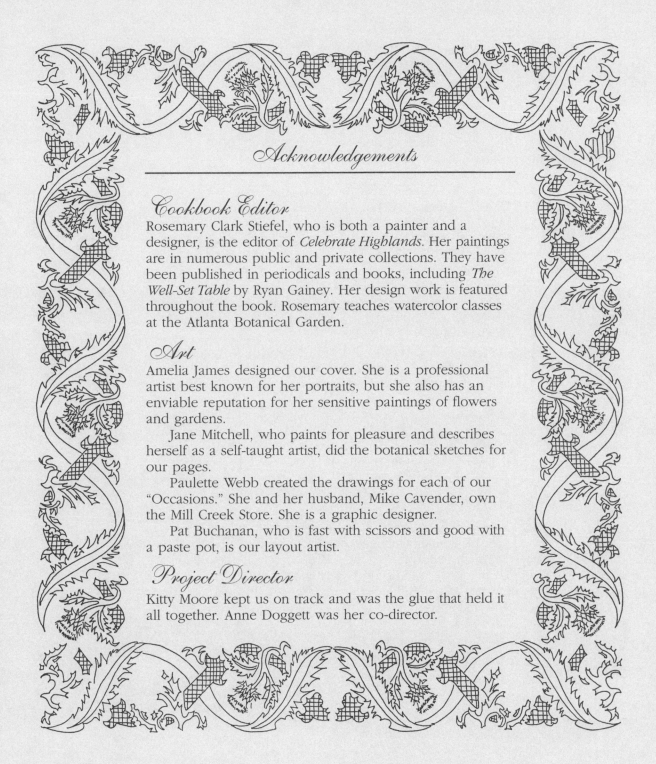

Acknowledgements

Cookbook Editor

Rosemary Clark Stiefel, who is both a painter and a designer, is the editor of *Celebrate Highlands*. Her paintings are in numerous public and private collections. They have been published in periodicals and books, including *The Well-Set Table* by Ryan Gainey. Her design work is featured throughout the book. Rosemary teaches watercolor classes at the Atlanta Botanical Garden.

Art

Amelia James designed our cover. She is a professional artist best known for her portraits, but she also has an enviable reputation for her sensitive paintings of flowers and gardens.

Jane Mitchell, who paints for pleasure and describes herself as a self-taught artist, did the botanical sketches for our pages.

Paulette Webb created the drawings for each of our "Occasions." She and her husband, Mike Cavender, own the Mill Creek Store. She is a graphic designer.

Pat Buchanan, who is fast with scissors and good with a paste pot, is our layout artist.

Project Director

Kitty Moore kept us on track and was the glue that held it all together. Anne Doggett was her co-director.

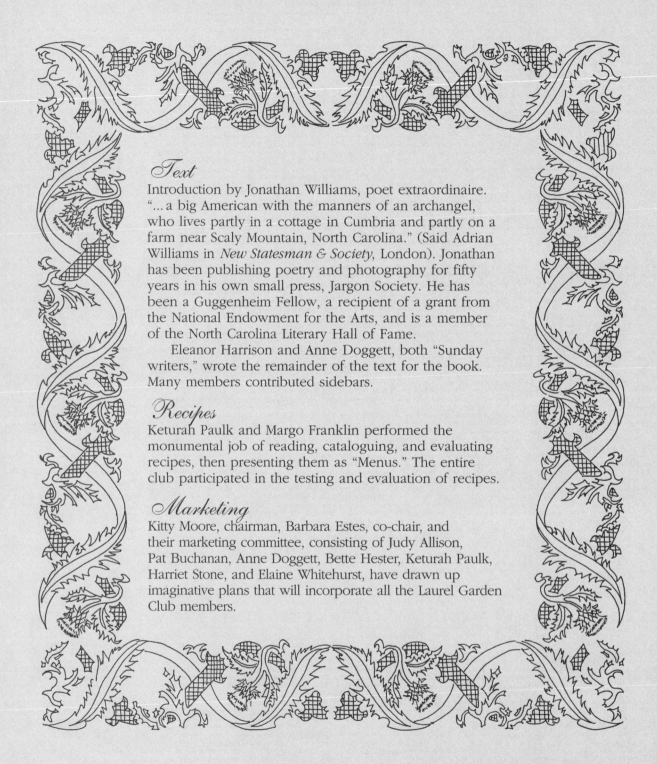

Text

Introduction by Jonathan Williams, poet extraordinaire.
"...a big American with the manners of an archangel,
who lives partly in a cottage in Cumbria and partly on a
farm near Scaly Mountain, North Carolina." (Said Adrian
Williams in *New Statesman & Society*, London). Jonathan
has been publishing poetry and photography for fifty
years in his own small press, Jargon Society. He has
been a Guggenheim Fellow, a recipient of a grant from
the National Endowment for the Arts, and is a member
of the North Carolina Literary Hall of Fame.

Eleanor Harrison and Anne Doggett, both "Sunday
writers," wrote the remainder of the text for the book.
Many members contributed sidebars.

Recipes

Keturah Paulk and Margo Franklin performed the
monumental job of reading, cataloguing, and evaluating
recipes, then presenting them as "Menus." The entire
club participated in the testing and evaluation of recipes.

Marketing

Kitty Moore, chairman, Barbara Estes, co-chair, and
their marketing committee, consisting of Judy Allison,
Pat Buchanan, Anne Doggett, Bette Hester, Keturah Paulk,
Harriet Stone, and Elaine Whitehurst, have drawn up
imaginative plans that will incorporate all the Laurel Garden
Club members.

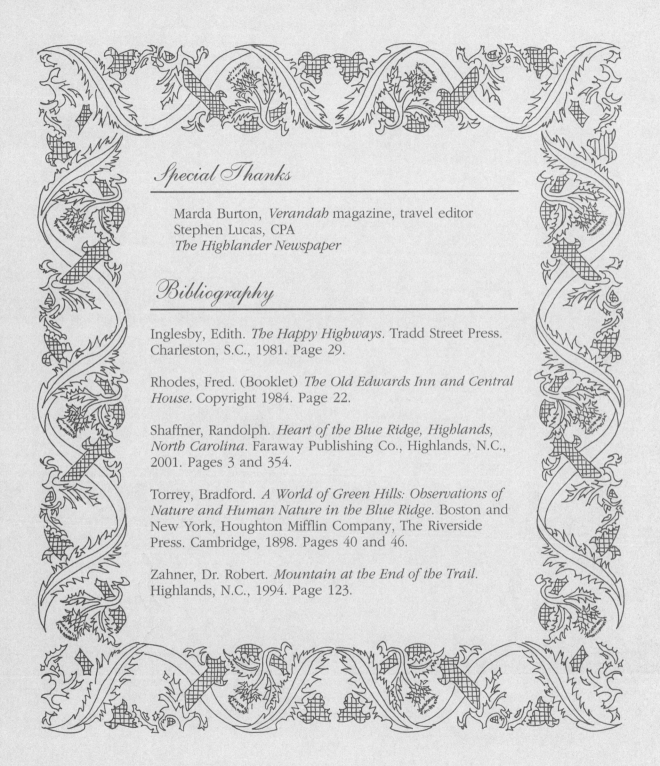

Special Thanks

Marda Burton, *Verandah* magazine, travel editor
Stephen Lucas, CPA
The Highlander Newspaper

Bibliography

Inglesby, Edith. *The Happy Highways*. Tradd Street Press. Charleston, S.C., 1981. Page 29.

Rhodes, Fred. (Booklet) *The Old Edwards Inn and Central House*. Copyright 1984. Page 22.

Shaffner, Randolph. *Heart of the Blue Ridge, Highlands, North Carolina*. Faraway Publishing Co., Highlands, N.C., 2001. Pages 3 and 354.

Torrey, Bradford. *A World of Green Hills: Observations of Nature and Human Nature in the Blue Ridge*. Boston and New York, Houghton Mifflin Company, The Riverside Press. Cambridge, 1898. Pages 40 and 46.

Zahner, Dr. Robert. *Mountain at the End of the Trail*. Highlands, N.C., 1994. Page 123.

Index

Accompaniments
Alan's Maniac Carib Spicy
   Mango Salsa, 147
Apple Butter, 114
Avocado Butter, 92
Black Bean and Corn Salsa, 78
Granola, 112
Horseradish Applesauce, 81
Lemon Thyme Butter, 76
Tabasco Mayonnaise, 95

Appetizers. *See also* Dips; Spreads
Antipasto Florida, 52
Bacon Crisps, 47
Bleu Cheese and Roasted
   Walnuts, 54
Bleu Cheese Torte with
   Sun-Dried Tomatoes and
   Pesto, 133
Cabin Onion Soufflé, 45
Cheddar Chili Cheesecake, 144
Chicken and Date Salad
   Canapés, 48
Chinese Chicken Wings, 48
Crab-Stuffed Mushrooms, 49
Fillet-Topped Baguettes, 46
Hot and Sweet Pecans, 55
Hot Chile Quesadillas, 53
Mexican Shrimp, 50
Mushroom Croustades, 140
Parmesan Pita Toasts, 113
Pesto Torta, 46
Shrimp Mousse Mold, 47
Smoked Salmon Appetizer
   Platter, 52
Sun-Dried Tomato Pesto and
   Shrimp Bruschetta, 51
Tortilla Pinwheels, 53

Apples
Apple Brownies, 126
Apple Butter, 114
Apple Harvest Cake, 122
Apple Torte, 120

Bleu Cheese and Roasted
   Walnuts, 54
Highlands Apples in a Dish, 151

Artichokes
Antipasto Florida, 52
Artichoke Rarebit, 110
Caviar Spread, 40
Curried Rice Salad, 66
Rainbow Pasta Salad, 66
Shrimp and Artichoke
   Casserole, 145
Wild Rice Pilaf, 101

Asparagus
Pasta with Sugar Snap Peas,
   Asparagus and Parmesan, 98
Roasted Sesame Asparagus, 67
Steamed Asparagus with Lemon
   Garlic Vinaigrette, 67

Bacon
Bacon Crisps, 47
Bleu Cheese Tomato Soup, 60
BLT Morning Pizza, 111

Beans
Black Bean and Corn
   Salsa, 78
Black Bean Dip, 40
Corn, Black Bean and Tomato
   Skillet, 69
Garlic Bean Soup, 137
Garlic Orange Couscous, 100
Haricots Verts with Parsley and
   Lemon Juice, 69
Mediterranean Lamb Stew, 149
Southwestern Bean Salad, 64
Southwestern Soup, 61
Tortilla Pinwheels, 53

Beef
Artichoke Rarebit, 110
Central House Meat Loaf, 134

Fillet-Topped Baguettes, 46
Grillades and Grits, 139
Grilled Flank Steak with Black
   Bean and Corn Salsa, 78
Roast Beef in Pita Pockets, 105

Beverages
Almond Tea, 55
Spicy Iced Tea, 56
Swedish Glögg, 56

Breads
Christmas Morning Rolls, 104
Cranberries and Cream
   Bread, 102
Rosemary Buttermilk
   Bread, 102
Sage Cream Biscuits, 103
Sour Cream Corn Bread, 103
Sweet Potato Biscuits, 104

Broccoli
Broccoli with Ripe Olive
   Sauce, 68
Rainbow Pasta Salad, 66

Brunch. *See also* Breads;
   Egg Dishes
Apricot Casserole, 114
Artichoke Rarebit, 110
BLT Morning Pizza, 111
Breakfast Oysters, 132
Giddy Up Grits, 111
Granola, 112
Parmesan Pita Toasts, 113
Sweet Onion Tart, 109
Tomato Basil Tart, 110

Cabbage
Colcannon (Cabbage and
   Potatoes), 71
Matchstick Vegetables with
   Lemon Thyme Butter, 76
Mustard Coleslaw, 61

Index

Cakes
Apple Harvest Cake, 122
Applesauce Cake, 135
Fig Preserve Cake, 123

Carrots
Garlic Bean Soup, 137
Lamb Shanks Deluxe, 80
Matchstick Vegetables with
    Lemon Thyme Butter, 76
Oven-Roasted Root Vegetables, 75
Pineapple Carrots, 68
Wild Rice Pilaf, 101

Chicken
Chicken and Date Salad
    Canapés, 48
Chicken Breast with Shrimp in
    Champagne Sauce, 83
Chicken Cutlets with
    Lime, 85
Chicken Tortilla Soup, 59
Chinese Chicken Wings, 48
Exotic Chicken with Thai
    Sauce, 84
Magnificent Marinated
    Chicken, 86
Quick and Easy Chicken
    Dubonnet, 85
Roast Chicken, 82
Thai Ginger Soup, 58

Cookies
Almond Cookies, 124
Lemon Biscotti, 138
Picnic Cookies, 124
Toffee Crunch Cookies, 125

Cookies, Bars
Amelia's Apricot Bars, 126
Apple Brownies, 126
Pecan Bars, 127
Pumpkin Bars, 128
Scotch Shortbread, 127

Corn
Black Bean and Corn
    Salsa, 78
Corn, Black Bean and Tomato
    Skillet, 69
Corn-for-Breakfast
    Casserole, 135
Mountain Corn Chowder, 142
Sour Cream Corn Bread, 103
Southwestern Bean Salad, 64
Southwestern Soup, 61

Crab Meat
Crab-Stuffed Mushrooms, 49
On the Verandah's
    Crabcakes, 146

Desserts. *See also* Cakes; Cookies
Apple Torte, 120
Boule de Neigh, 141
Chamber Music Sundaes, 118
Chocolate Cream Pots, 150
Cold Lemon Soufflé, 119
Fabulous Flan, 116
Fudge Pie, 136
Ginger Mousse, 118
Highlands Apples in a
    Dish, 151
Lemon Ice Cream, 117
Peach Ice Cream, 117
Peach Rum Soufflé, 120
Perfect Poached Pears, 116
Raspberry Walnut
    Torte, 121

Dips
Baked Mexican Spinach Dip
    with Tortilla Chips, 41
Black Bean Dip, 40
Greek Olive Tapenade, 42

Egg Dishes
Baked Eggs with Onions and
    Cheese, 108

Cheesy Jalapeño Pie, 109
Corn-for-Breakfast Casserole, 135
Southwestern Eggs, 108

Eggplant
Eggplant Soup, 138
Mediterranean Lamb Stew, 149
Portobello Mushroom Stacks, 70
Shrimp and Eggplant
    Casserole, 152

Fish. *See also* Salmon
Classic Bouillabaisse, 88
Crunchy Catfish, 89
Fish in a Dish, 94
Grilled Swordfish with Avocado
    Butter, 92
Mountain Trout (Three Ways), 93
On the Verandah's
    Crabcakes, 146
Tuna à la Dana, 94

Glazes/Icings/Toppings
Buttermilk Glaze, 123
Cream Cheese Icing, 128
Topping, 122

Grains
Cheese Grits, 87
Curried Rice Salad, 66
Garlic Orange Couscous, 100
Giddy Up Grits, 111
Green and Yellow Rice, 100
Grillades and Grits, 139
Rice and Green Chile
    Casserole, 101
Risotto ai Funghi Porcini, 147
Shrimp and Eggplant
    Casserole, 152
Wild Rice Pilaf, 101

Lamb
Lamb Shanks Deluxe, 80
Mediterranean Lamb Stew, 149

Index

Marinades/Rubs
Cajun Spice Rub for Fish, 95
Ginger Lime Marinade for
Swordfish, 96
Ginger Soy Marinade, 96

Mushrooms
Antipasto Florida, 52
Belvedere Mushroom Almond
Pâté, 43
Chicken Breast with Shrimp in
Champagne Sauce, 83
Crab-Stuffed Mushrooms, 49
Mushroom Croustades, 140
Portobello Mushroom
Stacks, 70
Risotto ai Funghi Porcini, 147
Roast Beef in Pita Pockets, 105
Shrimp and Artichoke
Casserole, 145
Wild Rice Pilaf, 101

Pasta
Greek Spaghetti, 142
Pasta with Sugar Snap Peas,
Asparagus and Parmesan, 98
Penne with Vodka and Spicy
Tomato Sauce, 99
Poached Salmon and Pasta with
Cucumber Dressing, 63
Rainbow Pasta Salad, 66

Peaches
Chilled Peach Soup, 58
Peach Ice Cream, 117
Peach Rum Soufflé, 120
Quick Pickled Peaches, 113

Pork. *See also* Bacon
Cheddar Chili Cheesecake, 144
Cold Oriental Loin of Pork with
Horseradish Applesauce, 81
Garlic Cilantro Grilled Pork
Tenderloin, 82

Giddy Up Grits, 111
Penne with Vodka and Spicy
Tomato Sauce, 99

Potatoes
Colcannon (Cabbage and
Potatoes), 71
Eggplant Soup, 138
Mediterranean Lamb Stew, 149
Oven-Roasted Root
Vegetables, 75
Whipped Potatoes with Garlic
and Chives, 72

Salad Dressings
Cucumber Dressing, 63

Salads
Almond and Orange Salad, 62
ASOA Salad, 145
Cucumber Ring, 65
Curried Rice Salad, 66
Mustard Coleslaw, 61
On the Verandah's Daikon
Pepper Slaw, 146
Poached Salmon and Pasta with
Cucumber Dressing, 63
Rainbow Pasta Salad, 66
Smoked Salmon on Salad
Greens, 62
Southwestern Bean Salad, 64
Spicy Tomato Aspic, 65
Tomato Cucumber Platter with
Feta, 64

Salmon
Grilled Salmon with Nasturtium
Butter, 141
Poached Salmon and Pasta with
Cucumber Dressing, 63
Salmon with Arugula, Tomato
and Caper Sauce, 90
Salmon with Creamy Lime
Sauce, 91

Smoked Salmon Appetizer
Platter, 52
Smoked Salmon on Salad
Greens, 62

Sandwiches
Roast Beef in Pita
Pockets, 105
U-Pick Tomato Sandwiches, 106
Vidalia Onion Sandwiches, 106

Sauces, Savory
Meat Loaf Glaze, 134
Orange Curry Sauce, 143

Seafood. *See also* Crab Meat;
Shrimp
Breakfast Oysters, 132
Classic Bouillabaisse, 88

Shrimp
Chicken Breast with Shrimp in
Champagne Sauce, 83
Classic Bouillabaisse, 88
Florida Gulf Coast BBQ
Shrimp, 86
Mexican Shrimp, 50
On the Verandah's
Crabcakes, 146
Shrimp and Artichoke
Casserole, 145
Shrimp and Cheese in Puff
Pastry with Orange Curry
Sauce, 143
Shrimp and Eggplant
Casserole, 152
Shrimp and Grits, 87
Shrimp Mousse Mold, 47
Sun-Dried Tomato Pesto and
Shrimp Bruschetta, 51

Side Dishes
Apricot Casserole, 114
Quick Pickled Peaches, 113

Index

Soups
Bleu Cheese Tomato Soup, 60
Chicken Tortilla Soup, 59
Chilled Peach Soup, 58
Eggplant Soup, 138
Garlic Bean Soup, 137
Marie's Chilled Cherry Soup, 136
Mountain Corn Chowder, 142
Southwestern Soup, 61
Thai Ginger Soup, 58
Tomato Florentine Soup, 148
Traveling Soup, 59

Spinach
ASOA Salad, 145
Baked Mexican Spinach Dip
    with Tortilla Chips, 41
Bleu Cheese Torte with
    Sun-Dried Tomatoes and
    Pesto, 133
Green and Yellow Rice, 100
Southwestern Soup, 61
Tomato Florentine Soup, 148

Spreads
Belvedere Mushroom Almond
    Pâté, 43
Brie with Apricot Spread, 44
Brie with Sun-Dried
    Tomatoes, 44
Caviar Spread, 40
Sherry Cheese Pâté, 42
Sun-Dried Tomato and Goat
    Cheese Spread, 45

White Pimento Cheese with
    Crackers, 41

Squash
Matchstick Vegetables with
    Lemon Thyme Butter, 76
Mediterranean Lamb Stew, 149
Portobello Mushroom Stacks, 70
Squash Gratin with White
    Cheddar Cheese, 75
Tomatoes Stuffed with
    Squash, 74

Tarts, Savory
Sweet Onion Tart, 109
Tomato Basil Tart, 110

Tomatoes
Baked Mexican Spinach Dip
    with Tortilla Chips, 41
Bleu Cheese Tomato Soup, 60
BLT Morning Pizza, 111
Corn, Black Bean and Tomato
    Skillet, 69
Garlic Orange Couscous, 100
Herb Baked Tomatoes, 72
Highlands Tomato Pie, 73
Mediterranean Lamb Stew, 149
Mexican Shrimp, 50
Penne with Vodka and Spicy
    Tomato Sauce, 99
Roast Beef in Pita Pockets, 105
Salmon with Arugula, Tomato
    and Caper Sauce, 90

Spicy Tomato Aspic, 65
Tomato Basil Tart, 110
Tomato Cucumber Platter with
    Feta, 64
Tomato Florentine Soup, 148
Tomatoes Stuffed with
    Squash, 74
U-Pick Tomato Sandwiches, 106

Veal
New Orleans Veal Scallops, 79

Vegetables. *See also* Artichokes;
    Asparagus; Beans; Broccoli;
    Cabbage; Carrots; Corn;
    Eggplant; Mushrooms;
    Potatoes; Spinach; Squash;
    Tomatoes; Zucchini
Matchstick Vegetables with
    Lemon Thyme Butter, 76
Oven-Roasted Root
    Vegetables, 75
Pasta with Sugar Snap Peas,
    Asparagus and Parmesan, 98

Zucchini
Mediterranean Lamb Stew, 149
Portobello Mushroom Stacks, 70
Tomatoes Stuffed with
    Squash, 74

Celebrate

HIGHLANDS

Recipes and Remembrance

Laurel Garden Club
P.O. Box 142
Highlands, North Carolina 28741
828-526-8134

YOUR ORDER	QUANTITY	TOTAL
Celebrate Highlands at $22.95 per book		$
North Carolina residents add 6.5% sales tax ($1.49)		$
Postage and handling at $4.00 per book		$
	TOTAL	$

Please make check payable to the Laurel Garden Club.

Name

Street Address

City   State   Zip

Telephone

Photocopies will be accepted.